Trail of the Coeur d'Alenes Unofficial Guidebook

And the 300k Bitterroot Loop

2016

by
Estar Holmes

Acknowledgement

This is the ninth edition of the *Trail of the Coeur d'Alenes Unofficial Guidebook*. The guide includes tips on riding the entire 300k Bitterroot Loop, as signed and mapped by the Friends of the Coeur d'Alene Trails. The loop comprises the Trail of the Coeur d'Alenes and the Route of the Hiawatha non-motorized trails, Northern Pacific and Milwaukee multi-use rail beds, and a 13-mile stretch of state highway.

This guide is a cooperative venture supported by more than sixty advertisers, book vendors, and information providers. My heartfelt thanks to all who participate in making the guide and related Web sites possible. Special thanks to Russ Davis of Gray Dog Press in Spokane, Washington, for his dedication in getting the book printed and distributed! Thanks to Mark Wagner, HDB Marine, for editing the manuscript.

Cover Photograph: Chatcolet Bridge and insert, Rick Shaffer, the "Prime Minister" of Wallace and the Trail of the Coeur d'Alenes.

Other Photo & Model Credits: pg. 5, Harrison Depot, courtesy of Crane Historical Society; pgs. 27 and 28, courtesy Margie Cantlon; pg. 30, Sorting Gap, courtesy museum of North Idaho; pg. 37, Crane girl, courtesy of Crane Historical Society; pg. 47, men in bateau, courtesy Museum of North Idaho; pg. 57, Silver Mountain Bike Park, Matt Vielle Photography ©2014 by permission of Silver Mountain; Silver Rapids Water Park, courtesy of Silver Mountain; pg. 81, Paul and Pat Aniotzbehere at Pulaski Trail; pg. 89, snowslide, courtesy Historic Wallace Preservation Society; pg. 93, Grand Forks, ID, courtesy Montana Historical Society Research Center Photograph Archives; pg. 102, Ferrell, courtesy Museum of North Idaho; pg.109, St. Maries waterfront, courtesy Museum of North Idaho.

Photography, compilation, graphic design, and book layout by Estar Holmes.

Enjoy many more pictures of the area traversed by the Bitterroot Loop at pinterest.com/bitterrootloop. You are encouraged to post pictures and comments about your rail-trail experiences on the *Trail of Coeur d'Alenes Riders* Facebook page. See what's happening on the Bitterroot Loop at facebook.com/Historic.Bitterroot.Loop. For updates on live music and lodgings in the greater south Lake CdA region, go to southlakecda.com.

Trail of The Coeur d'Alenes Unofficial Guidebook 2016
© 2016, South Lake Promotions, Inc., PO Box 185, Harrison, ID 83833

Published by
Gray Dog Press
Spokane, Washington
www.graydogpress.com
ISBN: 978-1-936178-98-8

Contents

Welcome
to North Idaho's
Trail of the Coeur d'Alenes
and the 300k Bitterroot Loop

This guide covers the popular Trail of the Coeur d'Alenes and connecting trails that comprise North Idaho's 300k Bitterroot Loop. Whether you plan to ride for a day or a week, it will help you plan your trip and enrich your appreciation of the history and culture of the area. Information for the guide is gathered by riding the trails, visiting communities, touring amenities, experiencing services, and speaking with the locals. If you are interested in a full cycle vacation check out the **Connecting Trips** selected for convenient cycle access and their unique offerings.

Most of the 300k loop is in the northern Idaho panhandle, with a short section in western Montana. The loop links the Trail of the Coeur d'Alenes, the Northern Pacific Route (Nor-Pac), Route of the Hiawatha (RoH), Milwaukee Scenic and Alternate Routes, and a 13-mile segment of rural highway along Idaho State Route-5 (SR-5).

The map on page 8 shows where the trails are situated in relation to the Spokane/Coeur d'Alene Metro Area. For more detailed maps, see the FAQ: *Where Can I Get a Map?*

Driving directions to trailheads and trailside communities are provided from I-90 because most people come to the trails with cycles on their vehicles. This guide, however, is focused on logistics for people who are traveling by cycle. The emphasis is on services and amenities that are conveniently located within a mile of the trails.

Also included are features that are within an easy ride from the main trails, or where courtesy shuttles are offered for you and your gear. Suggestions are included on ways to reach the Trail of the Coeur d'Alenes from as far away as Spokane International Airport by using a combination of dedicated cycling trails and public or private transportation. Alternatives to riding in traffic are offered wherever possible.

The guide has been released every year since 2008. It was inspired by John Kolby, owner of the former Pedal Pushers bike shop in Harrison, Idaho, a cycle mechanic extraordinaire, who was spending most of his time answering questions about the new Trail of the Coeur d'Alenes. He suggested the need for a book and the trail guide was born.

The Bitterroot Loop section was added after Friends of the Coeur d'Alene Trails volunteers mapped, signed, and linked the CdA Trail with three other railbed trails, and the 300k Bitterroot Loop was born. This trail network was featured in the *Rails to Trails Conservancy* magazine in 2010 and hundreds of cyclists started showing up on remote mountain roads, so it seemed like a good idea to let them know what to expect.

What's in this book?

After this introduction, you will see answers to **Frequently Asked Questions** and a **map** that shows where the Bitterroot Loop trails and **Connecting Trips** are situated. This is followed by descriptions of **trailheads** and **wayside stops**, and trailside **community tours**, interspersed with historical **points of interest** and **Connecting Trips**. Trailheads for the Trail of the Coeur d'Alenes and the entire Bitterroot Loop are listed in a clockwise direction starting at Plummer, Idaho.

Find quick references to resource suppliers starting at pg. 114, including **lodging and camping**, **rental shops**, and **transportation** services. This is also where to find phone numbers of trail managers and other officials. For convenient Web page links to the lodgings, restaurants, and downloadable maps, go to **southlakecda.com/trail.htm.**

People may wonder why certain offerings are included, or embellished upon, while others receive scant mention or none at all. Other than the obvious space and time constraints, it is more or less a matter of squeaky wheels. Attractions, activities, and amenities that appear on the writer's radar and seem interesting or useful to visitors are included. When business owners reach out and make their amentites available, they are likely to get more attention. Comments from the cycling community and others also influence what goes in or comes out. Cyclists are encouraged to share their own observations and insights on the *Trail of the Coeur d'Alenes Riders* Facebook page, or they can contact me privately via the information on the back of the title page.

Local business owners support the research, printing, and distribution of this guide through advertising. Those who show an interest in the book and the trail, and those who are hospitable, are more likely to inspire me to write about them. Businesses that make an extra effort to serve cyclists generally receive more attention than others. They want to cater to you. When making travel plans, please consider using their services.

Trail Conditions

The Trail of the Coeur d'Alenes is a well-maintained 72-mile ribbon of asphalt that spans the Idaho Panhandle from Plummer to Mullan.

Flooding caused a breach in the trail between Harrison and Cataldo in 2008

Check conditions on the Trail of the Coeur d'Alenes by calling headquarters at 208.682.3814 during business hours.

Weather events like downed trees or flooding may temporarily close parts of the trail occasionally.

The Trail of the CdA is paved but the rest of the Bitterroot Loop trails are packed dirt and gravel, with the exception of the13-mile asphalt stretch of State Route 5 (SR-5) between St. Maries and Heyburn State Park. The Trail of the Coeur d'Alenes and Hiawatha are dedicated non-motorized trails. The NorPac and Milwaukee are dirt roads shared with vehicles. The Milwauee will get dusty during dry spells.

The Trail of the Coeur d'Alenes is mostly flat except for 7-mile spans on either end. The approximate 5% grade between Plummer and Heyburn State Park, and on Chatcolet Bridge, are the steepest parts. The overall gain from the Lake Coeur d'Alene shoreline to Mullan, Idaho, is about 1,100 feet over a span of 60 miles. The most dramatic elevation changes occur on the NorPac section of the Bitterroot Loop between Mullan and Lookout Pass, where the trail climbs 1,461 feet in a little under 11 miles. Then the 37 miles between Lookout Pass and Avery descends 2,300 feet. On the RoH, a shuttle bus is available along the 1.7% incline back up the 15 mile-stretch between Pearson and Roland Trailheads.

A hybrid or mountain bike is suggested if you plan to ride the entire Bitterroot Loop. There are long dark tunnels in the mountainous sections, and helmets and lights are mandatory on the RoH. Be prepared for overnight wilderness survival in case of a mishap. Pack a repair kit, spare tubes, snacks,and plenty of water. There is no cell phone service in the remote areas. There are still land lines and a couple of pay phones along the way, so carry a prepaid phone card in your survival kit.

Welcome to North Idaho's Rail Trails

Connecting Trips

Since this guide focuses on the needs of visitors touring by cycle, emphasis is on facilities within one mile of the trails. However, *Connecting Trips* with fun amenities and interesting lodgings are featured if they are within an easy ride from the Bitterroot Loop, or accessible by courtesy shuttle or gondola.

Historic

The trails that comprise the Bitterroot Loop all lie within a portion of the aboriginal homeland of the Coeur d'Alene Tribe of Indians. The Trail of the Coeur d'Alenes follows the former Union Pacific rail line

You will need a good light for the tunnels along the Bitterroot Loop

that crossed ancient paths where the First People walked. The railroad cut through spectacular scenery traversed by mountain men, fur traders, Jesuit missionaries, soldiers, homesteaders, and fortune hunters who began arriving in the mid 1800s.

Bitterroot Loop trails follow the Northern Pacific and Old Milwaukee railbeds through rural areas that boomed when gold and silver were

Can you find this vestige of the old days on the trail between Plummer and Heyburn State Park?

discovered and lumber was king; where miners, loggers, and entrepreneurs—many of them first generation immigrants—flocked with hopes of creating better lives.

Visitors will find lots of history along these trails in the form of guided tours, interpretive signs, museums, murals, and books by local authors. The old stories cast a striking contrast between the optimistic attitudes of the tough settlers and the harsh realities of daily life during North Idaho's gold rush, logging days, and homesteading times. Old photographs and artifacts can be found at museums, of course, but many are also displayed on the walls of businesses and public buildings where visitors are welcome to have a look.

Point of Interest: The Native people here called themselves *Schitsu'Umsh*. It is believed French Canadian trappers called them *Coeur d'Alene*, and the name stuck. The first recorded encounter of tribal members and Caucasians occurred when a few of the *Schitsu'Umsh* traveled to Nez Perce country during Lewis & Clark's expedition to the Pacific Ocean. They met some of the explorers at an encampment, where they described their homeland and explained the size of their lake in terms of how many days it took to walk around it.

Scattered hunters and trappers filtered into the tribe's territory over the next few decades, but nobody can say exactly when they arrived. In 1842, the Jesuit missionary, Father Pierre DeSmet, S.J., built a log chapel near a tribal camp on the northern shore of Lake Coeur d'Alene at *Nchim Kinkw*, which means, Head of the Water.

The arrival of the priests had been eagerly anticipated by the *Schitsu'Umsh* for one hundred years. Their coming had been foretold by Chief Circling Raven, who received a vision that men with black robes and crossed sticks would come in peace with strong medicine. The need for strong medicine became critical after waves of smallpox ravaged the tribe and traditional healers were powerless against the deadly plagues. It is thought the *Schitsu'umsh* first became exposed to smallpox after horses were introduced to them in the 1700s, and their hunters mingled with other Indians during bison hunts south of here.

Protocol

The people of rural north Idaho are hospitable, hard working, and conservative. (The colloquialism "north Idaho" is preferred over "northern" Idaho). They consider extraction of natural resources, such as metal and wood, necessary for a quality life. They take pride in doing the hard and dangerous work of providing these raw materials to the market, and their heritage is defined by these occupations.

The Harrison train depot once serve about 1,000 people daily.

The locals miss the rumble and whistles of trains that came through several times a day. Those trains were a lifeline for many years, carrying ore, lumber, mail, supplies, and people between the wilds of Idaho and the civilized world. They meant goods were moving, money was being made, and people were able to provide for their families. Farmers could sell cream by putting a fresh container of it on a train bound for Spokane and come back a few days later to pick up the empty can. Those who couldn't afford train fare would walk along the tracks to get to distant towns.

The trains declined after highways were constructed, and the Inland Northwest became a die-hard motor culture. People love their quads, dirt bikes, snowmobiles, SUVs, and pickup trucks. Bicycles were not part of the transportation picture before the trail was established. In fact, the motorized locals are not at all accustomed to sharing "their" roads with cycles. Don't be surprised if they feel inconvnienced by having to slow down and go around people on bikes. If you decide to cycle on the rural highways, consider using a rear view mirror and hugging the edge of the pavement. You will find the roads have hardly any shoulders. That's not your fault, but most drivers in rural Idaho will figure there is something wrong with *you* if they have to swerve to get past you. That's one reason this book helps cyclists stick to the trails as much as possible.

The people of north Idaho love being out in the woods to hunt, fish, and pick mushrooms or huckleberries. Most would not consider doing this without some kind of firearm. In this day of concern about guns, visitors from more restrictive states should be aware that Idaho state law allows people to openly carry handguns and rifles in public. So, if you notice someone with a pistol holstered onto their belt or a rifle mounted in their pickup truck window, don't be alarmed. This is what perfectly respectable people do in Idaho. Don't worry, it is illegal to discharge a firearm in a state park unless there happens to be a shooting range there, or if there is an imminent threat to life and limb, and the Trail of the Coeur d'Alenes is the longest and narrowest state park in Idaho.

Speaking of laws, the State of Idaho is surrounded on all sides by governments that tolerate the use of marijuana to various degrees, but Idaho has some of the harshest anti-weed laws in the US. Medical marijuana cards from other states are not honored here. If you are traveling to Idaho from a pot-friendly state and cherish your freedom, consider leaving any marijuana and paraphernalia behind.

On the other hand, you may observe people in a couple of trailside communities wandering around the streets with alcoholic beverages in hand. The City of Wallace allows this, but only during one of the many events that occur around town, and the drink must be in a red cup, according to the folks at city hall. People also carry open containers in Harrison, where wandering around with a drink is a tradition not a right. There is an ordinance that prohibits the practice, but it is not often enforced.

While on the topic of protocol, word on the street is that some business owners are saying too many cyclists expect to use their restrooms or ask to have water bottles refilled without offering anything in return. So, to keep from embarassing yourself or others, please consider using the public facilities that are identified under the various trailhead sections.

A Constant State of Change

Businesses in rural north Idaho tend to be like wild mushrooms in that they come and go rather quickly. This guide attempts to keep up with the changing landscape, but businesses open, close, move, or change hands after publication. So, to stay safe and happy, it's best not to assume anything, call ahead, and remain flexible.

The Trail of the Coeur d'Alenes is well-managed by the Coeur d'Alene Tribe and the State of Idaho

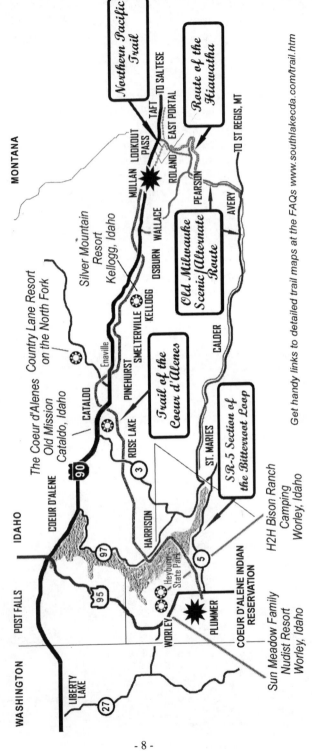

✸ The Trail of the Coeur d'Alenes and Connecting Trips ☼ on the 300k Bitterroot Loop

WASHINGTON

IDAHO

MONTANA

LIBERTY LAKE

POST FALLS

COEUR D'ALENE

Northern Pacific Trail

Route of the Hiawatha

TO SALTESE

TAFT

EAST PORTAL

LOOKOUT PASS

MULLAN

ROLAND

TO ST REGIS, MT

WALLACE

OSBURN

PEARSON

AVERY

Silver Mountain Resort
Kellogg, Idaho

Old Milwaukee Scenic/Alternate Route

KELLOGG

CALDER

SMELTERVILLE

Enaville

Country Lane Resort
on the North Fork

PINEHURST

CATALDO

The Coeur d'Alenes
Old Mission
Cataldo, Idaho

Trail of the
Coeur d'Alenes

ROSE LAKE

ST. MARIES

SR-5 Section of
the Bitterroot Loop

HARRISON

H2H Bison Ranch
Camping
Worley, Idaho

Heyburn State Park

WORLEY

PLUMMER

COEUR D'ALENE INDIAN RESERVATION

Sun Meadow Family
Nudist Resort
Worley, Idaho

Get handy links to detailed trail maps at the FAQs www.southlakecda.com/trail.htm

- 8 -

WHERE DOES THE TRAIL START?

Some say the trail starts in Mullan, Idaho, near the Montana border. Others consider Plummer, near the Washington state line, the beginning. This guide starts in Plummer for several reasons: The trail mile markers go from west to east; *Hn'ya(pqi'nn*, the Plummer trailhead, is closest to Spokane (the largest city between Seattle and Chicago); The Coeur d'Alene Tribe's headquarters are in Plummer, and both local history and the trail's establishment start with them. But with 19 trailheads, you can decide where to embark on your adventure.

HOW DO I GET TO THE TRAILHEADS?

Driving directions are provided from I-90 to each trailhead. Are you traveling without a vehicle? The FAQ: *How Do I Get to the Trail Without Driving?* explains how to reach the trail without a car, while avoiding riding in traffic as much as possible. See the entry, **Get to the Trails Without Driving,** in the **Bitterroot Loop Service Providers** section for ideas on private transportation options that will get you and your gear to a trailhead. Guests at the **Wallace Inn** may arrange for pick up by a paid shuttle from Spokane International Airport. Guests at the **Pines Motel** and **Fort Hemenway Manor** in St. Maries may request a courtesy shuttle between their lodgings and Heyburn State Park. Other possibilities include engaging a local tour company or shuttle service.

HOW MUCH DOES IT COST TO RIDE THE TRAIL?

Riding the Trail of the Coeur d'Alenes is free. There is no charge for parking at trailheads, except at Heyburn State Park, where it costs $5 per day, per vehicle. Idaho residents can get an annual pass for $10 when registering their vehicles, good at any state park for one year. Those who already registered vehicles but did not buy a park sticker can do so at any Idaho DMV. Nonresidents can buy an annual pass for $40.

Idaho resident veterans with a 100% service-related disability can apply for a lifetime Veteran's Pass that waives parking and basic camping fees. Get an application at any state park, park regional service center, or go online to parksandrecreation.idaho.gov/activities/camping click on *Discounts and Fees* in the left column. Then see *IdahoDisabled Veterans* and click *Apply Today*. This takes you to a brochure with the application.

Print, fill out, and fax or mail it to the address provided, along with a letter from the Idaho Department of Veteran's Affairs, affirming your disability. Call Heyburn State Park during business hours if you have questions about park fees: 208.686.1308.

HOW LONG DOES IT TAKE TO RIDE THIS TRAIL?

If you are in a big hurry, you can race across the Idaho Panhandle and back in a day. If you relish back country discoveries and moving in rural time, you can find enough to do and see to spend a relaxing and memorable week vacationing along the trail.

ARE TOURS AVAILABLE?

ROW Adventures offers a selection of guided tours for groups during the summer. Options include one day tours; 5-day package deals with a mix of cycling, rafting, and kayaking; and full logistical support for self-guided trail vacations. See *Local Trail Touring Service* on page 114.

WHAT ELSE IS THERE TO DO?

Hike, boat, float, kayak, stand up paddle, geocache, fish, mountain bike, swim, zipline, sight-see, taste wine, sip microbrews, dance, sing, golf, and more. Find things to do under each trailhead description, and check out the Connecting Trips for more ideas. Bike rides from the rail trails into the surrounding back country are documented by volunteers at: friendsofcdatrails.org/other_trails.html.

WHERE CAN I GET TRAIL MAPS?

Friends of the Coeur d'Alene Trails distributes maps to area businesses and visitor centers. You may also download their PDF or contact the Friends to request a map by mail. Find them at friends ofcdatrails.org or snail mail them at PO Box 804, Wallace, ID, 83873. The Friends map shows the entire 300k Bitterroot Loop. The State of Idaho provides an online map of the Trail of the Coeur d'Alenes only. It is in three segments that are printable on standard-sized paper. Easily find links to downloadable maps provided by both the Friends group and Idaho State Parks at southlakecda.com/trail. Look for the FAQ: *Where Can I Get a Map?* and click the "maps" link.

WHERE CAN I RENT CYCLES?

Cycle rentals are available along the Trail of the Coeur d'Alenes in

Harrison, Kellogg, and **Wallace.** You can find details about these shops and the cycles they specialize in under the trailhead community descriptions. Quickly access phone numbers in the *Service Providers* section in the back of the guide.

WHERE CAN I PITCH A TENT?

Caming along the trail right of way is not allowed. Several full service campgrounds are located on, or within a few blocks of the trail at: Heyburn State Park, Harrison, Cataldo, Kingston, Pinehurst, Osburn, and Wallace. See details about tenting and RV camping under trailhead listings. See back of book for phone numbers and southlakecda.com/trail.htm for links to campground Web sites.

ARE BONFIRES ALLOWED ALONG THE TRAIL?

Fires not allowed along the trail, only at campgrounds, except when there are restrictions due to dry conditions.

WHAT ABOUT LODGING?

There is a wide selection of lodgings and price ranges along the Trail of the Coeur d'Alenes, from rustic budget cabins to high end condos. You can find some really good deals on lodgings. Plan carefully along the rest of the Bitterroot Loop because it is rural and remote with overnight accommodations 25 miles or more apart.

WHAT KIND OF FOOD IS THERE ALONG THE WAY?

There are American, Mexican, and Chinese restaurants in communties along the trail. There are no vegetarian or vegan restaurants, but most provide a few meatless choices. Most cooks and chefs will attempt to feed people with vegetarian and vegan preferences, but don't expect them to have any special training in that area. When we are aware of vegan, vegetarian, gluten-free, organic, or locally grown options, they are noted under the individual restaurant descriptions. Quite a few restaurants make food from scratch with fresh ingredients and bake fresh daily. Wild huckleberries are prolific in the Northwest. Locals go on forays into the surrounding mountains to pick berries then sell them to restaurants, so you will find a wide variety of treats made from wild huckleberries. Organic and locally grown menu items are an exception not the rule on the loop. See **southlakecda.com/trail.htm** for a list of restaurants with menus online.

DO TRAILHEADS HAVE DRINKING WATER?

Trailheads and wayside stops do not have drinking water, with the exception of a fountain at *Hn'ya(pqi'nn* (Plummer) Trailhead. The only other water source that can be considered as "belonging to the trail," is a spigot east of Smelterville at the state owned shop next to the trail. Stretches between water sources vary from one to 25 miles, so stock up on fresh water whenever you can. You will ride along creeks, rivers, and lakes most of the way, but heavy metals from years of mining activity still wash into the drainage. Boiling this water in an attempt to purify it will just further concentrate metals. If you rely on a portable filter, be aware that large portions of the trail are flanked by private property so it's not always permissable to access lake and river water.

ARE RESTROOMS OPEN ALL YEAR?

Flush toilets at *Hn'ya)pqi'nn* Trailhead in Plummer shut down during cold weather to avoid damage from freezing. Vault toilets are open all year. The portable toilet at Cataldo is removed at the end of summer. There is no restroom at the trailhead in Wallace. Please use facilities at the Chamber of Commerce Visitor Centers, Northern Pacific Depot Museum, Wallace District Mining Museum, or the new Friend of the Coeur d'Alene Trails visitor center. Avoid using restrooms in businesses unless you intend to make a purchase.

ARE HELMETS REQUIRED?

Helmets are not legally required on the Trail of the Coeur d'Alenes or other trails of the Bitterroot Loop, with the exception of the Route of the Hiawatha, where they are mandatory.

HOW LONG MAY I PARK AT TRAILHEADS?

You may park long enough to ride the trail, except at Smelterville Trailhead, where overnight parking is banned. Expect an extra fee if parking overnight at Chatcolet Trailhead in Heyburn State Park.

IS THERE RV PARKING AT TRAILHEADS?

There are no designated RV parking spots at trailheads, but several have plenty of room to park and maneuver large rigs conveniently. These include: Plummer, Chatcolet, Silver Mountain, and Mullan. State and private RV parks close to the trails accommodate RVs at Heyburn, Harrison, Rose Lake, Cataldo, Enaville, Pinehurst, Kellogg, Osburn, Wallace, Lookout Pass, and along the St. Joe River. Find details under individual trailhead listings. See phone numbers under *Service Providers* and campground links at southlakecda.com/trail.htm.

WILL MY STUFF BE SAFE IN MY CAR AT TRAILHEADS?

There are no guarantees. This is a low-crime area, but lock valuables out of sight, just as you would anywhere. Police and sheriffs patrol trailheads in their jurisdictions. Contact officials in the jurisdictions listed in the back of the book if you want specific information.

IS THERE CELL PHONE COVERAGE?

Verizon and ATT cover the region with varying degrees of success. Service is spotty on the remote portions of the trail along the Coeur d'Alene River. Riders on the Bitterroot Loop should expect no service in the St. Joe River drainage to within about 10 miles of St. Maries.

IS THE TRAIL SAFE FOR WOMEN ALONE?

Women should take the same precautions as they do whenever traveling alone in a remote area.

ARE GROUP PERMITS REQUIRED?

Yes. Groups of 25 or more are required to contact a trail manager to request a permit. Additionally, any group wishing to host a special event or commercial activity on the trail must have authorization from trail managers. Find their phone numbers under: *Information About Area Cycle Trails* in the *Bitterroot Loop Service Providers* section.

CAN I BRING MY DOG?

Pets are welcome on the trail as long as they remain on a short leash and under your control at all times. Please clean up any "land mines" they deposit.

CAN I BRING MY HORSE?

Horses are not allowed on the trail.

WHAT IS THE BEST SEASON TO RIDE?

If you crave solitude, ride in spring or late fall. The scent of blooming wildflowers is a big treat in spring. However, some businesses may still be in winter hibernation mode or on seasonal hours then. To experience everything trailside communities have to offer, come between Memorial and Labor Days. Summertime temperatures are generally pleasant, but there can be scorchers reaching into the 100s. October offers a spectacular display of vibrant colors, and average Indian summer temperatures are in the high 50s and 60s. Winter conditions vary widely in north Idaho from year to year. Snow generally starts around Thanksgiving and stays until March. There may be brief snowstorms in April or even May.

IS THERE CROSS-COUNTRY SKIING?

You are welcome to ski on the trail. The amount of snow varies from year to year and location on the trail. The parks department sets track around Smelterville when conditions allow. It snows more between Wallace and Mullan, and this section is shared with snowmobiles. Call 208.682.3814 for updates.

CAN I GET HELP IF I CRASH MY BIKE?

If a mishap renders your bike inoperable, what should you do?

Jason Brown of the Coeur d'Alene Tribe's Recreation Department says, "I would view those types of issues similar to hiking in a remote area. You should always go with someone else in the event something happens, so that person can go for help." That's good advice, but if you decide to ride alone anyway, keep this guide with you. It lists telephone numbers of transportation companies and trail managers you can call if you happen to be at a spot with cell service. If someone is hurt, dial 9-1-1.

Otherwise, you're on your own or at the mercy of a kind passerby. Or, you can ride with peace of mind by hiring **ROW Adventures**, which offers self-guided trail vacations with full, 24-hour logistical support.

Some people have crashed into the **bollards** that are placed at cross-roads to warn of possible vehicle traffic. Note the squiggly white lines before them and the stop signs on them. To avoid slamming into a bollard or being hit by a car, it's best to slow down and stop.

IS THE TRAIL ADA ACCESSIBLE?

Trailheads have marked disabled parking spaces and most have accessible restrooms, except for the portable potties at two trailheads. Please refer to trailhead descriptions for details.

ARE MOTORIZED VEHICLES ALLOWED?

The CdA Trail is non-motorized with the exception of a multi-use section between Wallace and Mullan, open to snowmobiles during winter. You will occasionally encounter official trail vehicles along the way. Motorized wheelchairs are freely allowed on the trail. Anyone with a disability who wants to use another type of motorized device, such as an electric bike, needs a permit. Go in person to Heyburn Park, the Old Mission, or the Coeur d'Alene Tribe, and ask for the trail manager. There is no charge for the permit, but you will be required to indicate you are disabled. Call first to inquire what devices are allowed and to make sure someone is available to issue the permit.

WHAT WILDLIFE IS THERE?

Much of the trail is rural, and one of its charms is the presence of wild animals. Eagle, osprey, blue heron, deer, beaver, snake, turtle, turkey, moose, coyote, bear, elk, and cougar all live in the region. Do not attempt to feed or otherwise befriend any wild animals. If you see a cute little baby do not try to pet it. Assume a protective mother is nearby ready to attack you. Give all wild animals plenty of room to get away from you. Please report bear, cougar, or moose sightings within the Coeur d'Alene Indian Reservation to the tribal wildlife program by calling 208.686.6603. You may call trail managers on weekdays to get updates on animal sightings and any other trail information that involves your safety.

WHAT'S WITH THOSE WARNING SIGNS?

Heavy metals from more than a century of mining are still being isolated and cleaned up in the Coeur d'Alene River drainage. Several factors contribute to their presence: Mining companies did not historically isolate tailings from the environment, so they wash down through the Coeur d'Alene River drainage; portions of the rail bed were built with mine waste; and ore sometimes spilled from passing trains. The asphalt strip, basalt armoring, gravel, and plants along the trail are there to cover metals remaining in the soil. The EPA has declared the trail safe for public use. Many locals are convinced there was never a danger in the first place, and that the federal government is blowing things out of proportion for its own sinister ends. The view on the Coeur d'Alene Reservation is different. The tribe insisted on removal of all contaminants feasible from along the railroad grade.

HOW DO I GET TO THE TRAIL WITHOUT DRIVING?

This FAQ is for cycle travelers coming from as far as Spokane International Airport, who want to get to the trail while avoiding riding in traffic as much as possible.

You can hire **ROW Adventures** to pick you up at the airport and handle all trail travel logistics for you. They offer a several options so, see *Getting to the Trails Without Driving* in the **Service Providers** section.

Guests who lodge at the **Wallace Inn** may request a paid shuttle for themselves and their cycles from Spokane International Airport to the motel. Shuttle arrangements must be made at least two weeks in advance.

Spokane Airport Express shuttles people and cycles to and from anywhere in the region, so don't let the "airport" part of their name stop you from calling. It is best to provide at least two days advance notice if possible, and more if you have a large group. However, they will try to accommodate people who need rides with a shorter lead time if possible, so it doesn't hurt to call and ask. If you need transport give them a call at 509.413.7986.

Captain Lou's Bicycle Shuttle Service provides car shuttles for people and cycles. Lou can pick up and deliver to Trail of the Coeur d'Alenes trailheads, Route of the Hiawatha, Coeur d'Alene, and Spokane International Airport. Call or text 208.818.2254 to discuss your options.

If you don't want to pay a service to get you to the trail from Spokane, you can cycle to Coeur d'Alene on recreational trails and ride the bus (still free as of this writing) the rest of the way to Plummer Trailhead.

If coming from the airport, catch Spokane Transit Authority bus #60 from Spokane Airport to the Bus Plaza, downtown Spokane. (Helmets are required in Spokane.) From the Bus Plaza, ride east one block on Riverside, and four blocks north on Howard. Enter Riverfront Park and look for the Spokane Centennial Trail markings on the ground next to the carousel. Ride this paved and mostly flat trail east about 38 miles to downtown Coeur d'Alene, Idaho.

You can eliminate 16 miles of biking by taking a bus through the Spokane Metro Area. Board the #174 Liberty Lake Express at the Bus Plaza and ride it to the end of the line at Liberty Lake. From there, you can pick up the Spokane Centennial Trail at Harvard Trailhead, an easy 1.3 miles north on Harvard Rd. The Idaho state line is five miles east. The trail turns into the North Idaho Centennial Trail and continues through Post Falls, Idaho, to Coeur d'Alene.

The Centennial Trail leads to the CityLink bus stop at Riverstone. Buses leave Riverstone for the **Coeur d'Alene Casino** near Worley, Idaho, every 85 minutes. Change buses at the casino for the Rural Route that will drop you off at the Plummer Trailhead. After a long day of riding trails and buses, rest up at the casino and get a fresh start to Plummer in the morning. CityLink buses carry from two to four cycles on a first-come-first-served basis, so be sure to arrive early. See both STA and CityLink Web sites for schedules and instructions on how to ride the bus with a cycle.

There is also the option of cycling to Coeur d'Alene, then chartering a boat and driver to take you to Harrison Trailhead. Call or text HI Water Adventures at 208-582-0177.

Hn'ya'(pqi'nn Trailhead (Gathering Place)

DRIVING DIRECTIONS: From I-90 take Hwy 95 (Sandpoint/Moscow exit) south 31 miles to Plummer. Turn right on Anne Antelope Rd. to trailhead parking.

TRAILHEAD AMENITIES: Restroom/Accessible (seasonal), Water, Picnic Area, Trail Info, 80 Parking Spaces/5 ADA. Please park RVs in the west section of the parking area. CityLink Bus Stop. (Food, Lodging, Swimming, Shopping, Showers, Post Office nearby). **Next Stop: 2.4 miles**

Warrior statue at Hn'ya'(pqi'nn Trailhead

Plummer, Idaho ELEVATION: 2,767 FT.

The City of Plummer, pop. 1,017, is the headquarters of the Coeur d'Alene Tribe. The trailhead is part of the Coeur d'Alene Tribe's *Hoy ch'ulte'lqu'lmkhw* **Veteran's Memorial Park**. The name denotes the Coeur d'Alene's interpretation of what it means to return back home after being at war. Fifteen miles of the trail traverse the Coeur d'Alene reservation and the tribe manages that portion. Trailheads on the reservation are named in the Coeur d'Alene language, and you will see historical markers that commemorate places and events significant to the tribe. *(See Coeur d'Alene languge Pronunciation Key, page 21)*

Hoy ch'ulte'lqu'lmkhw Veteran's Memorial Park, Plummer, Idaho.

Plummer, Idaho

South, across the field from the trailhead, you can see the modern Coeur d'Alene Tribal **Wellness Center**. The public is welcome on a drop-in basis to enjoy the large **pool, spa, steam room**, and **exercise equipment**. Cost is $5 for adults and $2 for children 6 to 18. Showers only are $2. Summer pool hours are 6:30 a.m. to 6:45 p.m. weekdays, Sat. from 8:30 a.m. to 1:45 p.m., and Sun 11:30 a.m. to 5:45 p.m. Call 208.686.9355 for seasonal and pool hours. To avoid riding on Hwy. 95, exit on the west side of the trail parking area, head south, then turn left on "A" Street.

The Warpath gift shop borders Hwy. 95 just past the Wellness Center. It's the only place along the trails to get **gifts** with a Native American theme. The collection includes moccasins, sandals, Pendleton jackets, sweat shirts, music by tribal musicians, Indian jewelry, beads, leather, and other regalia supplies. **Plummer Hardware** is on the south side of the building. They have a small section of camping supplies and a few emergency bike parts like tubes and locks.

The **Gateway Café**, across the street on the corner of Hwy. 95 and "A" Street, is where the locals go for a hearty breakfast, lunch, or dinner. Omelettes, huckleberry pancakes, wraps, homemade soups, a salad bar, burgers, and sandwiches are a few items on the menu. Desserts include huckleberry specialties, such as ice cream, cheesecake, and home baked pies. They will gladly pack a sack lunch for you to enjoy along the trail.

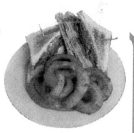

Plummer, Idaho

Benewah Market is a tribally-owned **full service grocery** store next to Highway 95, a block south of the Gateway Café. You will find a

Market Bistro, a **bakery**, and a wide variety of items, incuding: hard **ice cream,** fresh fruits and vegetables, fresh meat cut on site, and any other groceries you may want to stock up on for the trail. This is also a place to get **bottled water**, energy bars, and any last minute needs.

The bakery proudly features a treat you won't find elsewhere for miles around: freshly prepared **donuts** fried in-house daily, or try our signature cinnamon rolls! We aso decorate cakes.

The bistro offers **breakfast biscuits**, burritos, fried chicken, fresh salads, and **sub sandwiches** made your way on bread baked in the store.

Other services include **Western Union**, money orders, **ATM**, DVD rentals, and phone cards. **The CityLink bus** stops right out front. Inquire at the courtesy desk for departure times.

The Ace hardware store has a **small bicycle section** and most items found at an Ace hardware store, such as housewares and some **camping accessories.** We also sell fishing and hunting supplies. There are no more stores along the trail until Harrison, so consider stocking up in Plummer.

Full Service Grocery and Hardware Store

Sandwiches & Donuts Prepared Fresh Daily

Summer Hours 7 am to 9 pm
Winter Hours 7 am to 8 pm

208-686-1216 ~ Hwy 95 & B St. in Plummer, Idaho

Plummer, Idaho

Point of Interest: The Coeur d'Alene Tribe's aboriginal territory covered more than four million acres, from meadows west of here to the mountains in the east. Lake Coeur d'Alene was the crown jewel central to tribal society. In the late 1880s news of gold, silver, and vast stands of timber caused a stampede of strangers to the area. Soon, those who had lived here since time immemorial were considered to be in the way of progress. As pressures of encroachment mounted, priests at the Old Mission convinced some tribal leaders that a reservation with clear boundaries would be the tribe's best hope for survival. A reservation was established for exclusive tribal use, but in 1909, the US government reneged on its agreement and threw the reservation open to homesteaders. This resulted in cultural upheaval and economic hardship for tribal families, and a "checkerboard" pattern of land ownership and legal jurisdictional confusion that still causes consternation to this day. Despite the problems that come with being colonized, the Coeur d'Alene tribe has risen to prominence in the region. They are among north Idaho's top employers, and share their success through generous contributions to education, health care, and public transportation that benefit people both on and off the reservation.

COEUR D'ALENE LANGUAGE PRONUNCIATION KEY

hn'ya'(pqi'nn	Gathering Place
hn-tsaq-aq-n	Stopping Place
hn-pet-pt-qwe'n	Place for Racing
hn-dar-ep	Canoe Landing
sqwe'-mu'-lmkhw	A Familiar Place

In general, the hyphens indicate the separation of significant parts (prefixes, verb roots, suffixes), but they also fit pretty neatly into syllable breaks. The stressed syllable has the vowel bolded.

The *hn-* prefix means 'place,' and is pronounced something like (Atilla the) hun, or hin(ge), or hen(-house), but without much of a vowel in the middle. It's closer to a schwa.

In the way that the tribe chooses to represent these sounds, there is no schwa (upside down 'e'), but you can probably imagine what it sounds like by noticing that it belongs before *n, m, r, l*, as in the last syllable of *'button, item, actor, level.'*

Each *'e'* above sounds like the vowel in *pet, bet, get, bed*, etc. All of the *'a'* sounds rhyme with *saw, wad, odd, pod*, etc. The *'i '* is like a long-e, *'mean, feed, fiend, army, machine.'*

Pronunciation key courtesy of the Coeur d'Alene Tribe Language Program

Plummer, Idaho

The **post office** is around the corner from Benewah Market on Hwy. 95. Go south another block to the junction with SR-5 for the **Hiway Motel,** Plummer's only lodging option. If you plan to fish along the trail, you can get **licenses** there.

Rising Star Espresso stand, one more block south on Hwy. 95, opens early daily. They serve hot and cold **coffee drinks**, teas, granitas, and chai. They have almond milk and soy milk options, and fresh fruit smoothies. The jalapeno bagel with cream cheese is a local favorite. The baristas make specialty drinks by request, and they give out Trail of the Coeur d'Alenes **maps** when available.

Ride east on "D" Street two blocks to 8th Street, to the **Plummer Public Library**. They open Mon. through Wed., 10 a.m. to 6 p.m., Thurs. 2 to 6 p.m. and Sat. 10 a.m. to 2 p.m. Public access computers are available for 30 minutes at a time on a drop-in basis, or longer when reserved.

Point of Interest: This is the vicinithy of Plummer's original settlement, of which barely anything remains. When homesteaders arrived in 1910, they found an old growth Ponderosa pine forest so thick and tall the sun barely shone through. The trees were cut down by hand to make room for tent sites and the first Old West style buildings. Tree removal was a major occupation in those early days and the wealth of timber in the area kept at least three sawmills operating day and night.

Turn north on 8th, at the Library to find **AVUBAH:** A Very Unique Boutique and Antique House, in the brightly painted old house a half block north. Cyclists are welcome to picnic in the shady yard.

Plummer, Idaho

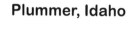

A Very Unique Boutique & Antique House

The two-story boutique and collectibles shop is a great place to pick up **locally made jams, jellies, jewelry, art,** and **soaps.** Cycle visitors are welcome to stop in with questions about the area. Bring a picnic, park your ride at the green bike rack out front, and relax in the shady yard, or catch up on your email on the free Wifi. Get **bottled water** and **trail maps** when available.

336 8th St. in Plummer
avubah.wordpress.com
See us on Facebook

Hours change with the seasons, so call when making your plans
208.661.6313

Plummer, Idaho

Point of Interest: The dilapidated white building across from AVUBAH is the old City Market, one of the few remaining relics of what was once a bustling business district with wooden sidewalks that provided some respite from the muddy streets of historic Plummer.

Bobbi's famous rez bar, is next to AVUBAH. "Famous" for its part in Sherman Alexie's Native American classic, *Smoke Signals*. Many locals acted as extras in the film. People drop in just to see the peavys, chokers, and saws on the walls, that are reminders of the area's logging heritage. An avid supporter of live music, especially the blues, Bobbi's hosts bands on selected weekends. Upcoming acts are posted at facebook.com/Bobbis.Bar. Pizzas, egg rolls, and assorted boxed dinners are available daily until 1 a.m. at this full-service lounge.

Point of Interest: Bobbi's is one of the oldest remaining buildings in town. It got its start as Frank McCaslin's Plummer Mercantile in 1914. Through the years it also served as the American Legion Hall, a supper club called the Pink Sarang, and the Main Street Mill bar. It is the site of the town's first water well, which was drilled out back by the building's original owner. The townspeople flocked here with jugs and buckets to collect fresh water for their daily needs. Before that, heavy buckets had to be carried from springs near Plummer Butte or Plummer Creek. Hobos and other itinerants traveling through by railroad would often be hired to haul water for a few cents.

When you are ready to start your journey, proceed from the trailhead through the tunnel and ride along the outskirts of Plummer for about a mile, before being treated to a scenic six-mile descent through Plummer Canyon. The trail follows an old Indian footpath that was part of an ancient network that led to the Rocky Mountains and beyond. Bear sightings are fairly common along this stretch of the trail.

Hn-tsaq-aq-n Scenic Wayside (Stopping Place) Trail Miles: 2.7

WHERE AM I?
Overlooking Plummer Creek on the Coeur d'Alene Indian Reservation.

REST AREA AMENITIES: Restroom/Accessible, Picnic Table, Interpretive Sign.
Next Stop: 1.8 miles

Hn-pet-pt-qwe'n Scenic Wayside (Place for Racing)
Trail Miles: 4.5

WHERE AM I?
Plummer Canyon on the Coeur d'Alene Indian Reservation.

REST AREA AMENITIES: Restroom/Accessible, Picnic Table, Interpretive Sign.
Next Stop: 1.7 miles

Trail Miles: 6.2 **Indian Cliffs Trailhead**

DRIVING DIRECTIONS: From I-90 take HWY 95 south 32 miles to SR-5. Head east six miles and turn left on Chatcolet Rd. Stop at the office for a parking permit. Indian Cliffs Trailhead is 1.2 miles on the left, but the small parking area there is reserved for Indian Cliffs hikers. Trail parking is 1.3 miles ahead at Chatcolet Trailhead.

TRAILHEAD AMENITIES: Interpretive Sign, Hiking Trails, (Restroom/Accessible, Water, Picnic Area, Lodging, Camping, Swimming, Rentals, Showers nearby)

Deer in Heyburn State Park   **Next Stop: 1.3 miles**

ELEVATION: 2,128 FT.   **Heyburn State Park/Heyburn Park**

(The State of Idaho refers to this area as Heyburn State Park. The Coeur d'Alene Tribe calls it Heyburn Park. Both references are used within the co-managed area).

Heyburn is Idaho's oldest state park. It has 26 miles of **trails** for hikers, mountain bikers, and horseback riders. The hiking trail at Indian Cliffs Trailhead is about three miles, moderate to steep. Watch for wildlife as the trail ascends through scenic stands of pine, fir, cedar, hemlock, and Pacific yew. From the top you can get a good view of the St. Joe River and lakes that converge in the park for your boating, fishing, and swimming pleasure. An easy to moderate one-mile CCC Nature Trail intersects Indian Cliffs Trail near the trailhead.

For **Park headquarters** and Hawley's Landing **campground**, take Chatcolet Rd. south (right) for 1.2 miles. There is a **restroom** at the **Plummer Marsh** area along the way. Pay fees, get **visitor information, trail maps,** and nature guides at headquarters.

Overnight accommodations in the park include **tent and RV camping,** rustic **cabins,** and two-bedroom **cottages** that sleep up to eight people. Cabins and cottages are available year round and there is a three-night minimum stay. Lodgings in the park are in high demand, especially during summer, so make reservations early online at parksandrecreation.idaho.gov, or call. 888.922.6743.

Plummer Marsh, Heyburn Park

Heyburn State Park/Heyburn Park

Hawley's Landing campground next to park headquarters has **free interpretive programs** all summer, such as crafts, nature walks, and guided **canoe trips**. There are free showers for campers. Day visitors can **shower for $3**.

Point of Interest: Many birds nest in the park, including 50 pair of opsrey. You may request a list of birds at park headquarters.

If you are riding the entire Bitterroot Loop in a counterclockwise direction, the 13-mile highway portion to St. Maries starts at the park entrance. The route is a two-lane rural commuter route with scant shoulders and quite a bit of uphill pedaling. Courtesy shuttles between here and St. Maries are offered to guests who stay at the **Pines Motel** or **Fort Hemenway Manor**. This guidebook takes the clockwise route, so we'll be visiting St. Maries later, on page 103.

Dry cabin at Heyburn Park

As you continue toward Chatcolet Trailhead from Indian Cliffs, you can see the Osprey and Heron **camping cabins** tucked into the trees to your left .2 mile down the trail. They have power, but water and vault toilet are outside. Cabins include a microwave and sleep 3 (with bunk). Bring your own bedding. Watch for the path on the right. It leads to Plummer Point, with a nice secluded **picnic** shelter and **swimming** beach. There is a **water fountain** as well.

Chatcolet Trailhead   Trail Miles: 7.5

DRIVING DIRECTIONS: From I-90 take HWY 95 south 32 miles to SR-5. Head east six miles and turn left at the park entrance onto Chatcolet Rd. Stop at the office for a parking permit, $5/day MVEF parking fee. Drive 2.5 miles north. Bear right at the fork and go downhill toward the large parking area next to the lake.

TRAILHEAD AMENITIES: Public Restroom/ Accessible, Water (seaonal). Picnic Area, Trail Info, Swimming. 100 Parking Spaces/none ADA marked. Large unpaved parking lot with plenty of room for RVs. (Lodging, Camping, Hiking nearby). Camping is only allowed in designated campgrounds, but vehicles may be left at the trailhead for an additional $5.30 per night while you ride the trails. Inquire at headquarters.

Next Stop: 2.5 miles.

Heyburn State Park/Heyburn Park

There is a **tent campground** up the hill behind the Chatcolet day use **picnic area**. Cycles can be walked to the campground from the Trail of the Coeur d'Alenes on a grassy trail between the parking area and Chatcolet bridge. Otherwise it's a steep half-mile climb by road from the parking lot. In that case, head uphill, bear right through the fork and continue past the private homes and **Chatcolet**

Chacolet Bridge in Heyburn State Park

Rental Cabin to the tent area. There is a host at the campground during summer. You can also check yourself in at the sign, but advance reservations are highly recommended via reserveamerica.com. **Firewood** is available for purchase.

Point of Interest: Hike along a portion of the **historic Mullan Road** from the interpretive sign at the tent campground. Capt. John Mullan and his crew were here in 1859 chopping and hacking a 624-mile swath from Walla Walla, Washington, to the Missouri River. They constructed a "corduroy" log bridge from the shore to the St. Joe River. This branch of the Mullan road was later abandoned for a drier route to the

north—the present day I-90. But many determined gold seekers, loggers, and backwoods entrepreneurs continued to use this old Mullan trail to access the St. Joe River country to the east.

Chatcolet Bridge was originally designed to swing open for steamboats cruising the St. Joe River. It was retrofitted to become one of the trail's most striking features. The stair step design makes the ascent easier, and the descent fun.

Chatcolet Lake, Hidden Lake, Round Lake, and the southern end of Lake Coeur d'Alene, all lie within the park. Flooding caused by the Post Falls Dam makes them look like one big lake.

The Chatcolet Trailhead parking lot is the point from which courtesy shuttles are offered for two **Connecting Trips** up the hill to the west.

family nudist resort

A unique connecting trip and safe alternative for women travelers is 3.5 miles from Chatcolet Trailhead at the gated **Sun Meadow Family Nudist Resort**. Getting there requires a steep 1.4-mile climb from Chatcolet Trailhead, so cycling guests should inquire about a **courtesy shuttle** from the trailhead when making reservations.

The resort has a main lodge with **large indoor pool, fitness center, recroom, library**, free wireless Internet, and **hotel rooms** with private bathrooms. People gather in the multipurpose hall with big screen movies, dancing, and **live music** acts by national artists. Nutritious **home cooked meals** are served to guests daily and the cook is happy to accommodate special dietary needs. Inquire about morning **yoga**, pool exercises, and **massages**.

The grounds include 69 full-service **RV sites, cabin**, pet-friendly RV, and shady **tent area**. There is an **outdoor pool, hot tub**, playground, bocce court, volleyball court, pond, and **hiking** trails. Advance reservations are encouraged but not required. Are you new to social nudism? Call the friendly SunMeadow staff with all your questions or concerns.

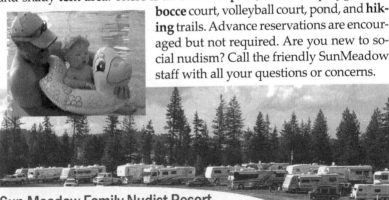

Sun Meadow Family Nudist Resort
sunmeadow.org   30400 S. Sunray Trail, Worley, Idaho 83876   **208.686.8686**

Camp with the Bison

Experience another unique Connecting Trip at the **H2H Bison Ranch**, where buffalo roam on 35 forested acres. The camp is just 3.5 miles west of Chatcolet Trailhead and offers eight full service **RV sites,** a cozy **tipi,** and **camping cabins** with beds, mini-fridge and coffee pot. New this year are indoor shower house, laundry facility, and restroom. People traveling light by cycle may arrange for bedding to be supplied in the cabins. Guests are free to use the **barbecue** and "pit kitchen," complete with modern appliances. Request groceries to be waiting when you arrive so you don't have to worry about packing food. Relax around the **bonfire,** where owners Buzz and Melissa will share **stories** about the fascinating bison. It's a steep climb from Chatcolet Trailhead, so when making reservations, inquire about a **courtesy shuttle** for two or more guests.

h2hbisonranch.com
208.659.6308
h2hbisonranch@gmail.com

H2H BISON RANCH

30585 S. Ditmore Rd,
Worley, Id 83876

Lake Coeur d'Alene

Point of Interest: The St. Joe River empties into Lake Coeur d'Alene where the navigational light marks its mouth, slightly north of Chatcolet Bridge. A string of buildings stood on the eastern riverbank before it was submerged by the Post Falls Dam. This was the site of the St. Joe Boom Company Sorting Gap, which became a frenzied hub of activity each year during the spring thaw, when some 40 million feet of timber floated out of the mountains via the great log drives on the St. Joe River. There was a cookhouse, bunkhouse, and shops on pilings, plus a system of sorting jacks and booms. The logs were branded in the woods when the trees were cut for various companies, then mixed

The Western, St. Joe, and Samson at the Sorting Gap, St. Joe River, c. 1910. Photo courtesy Museum of North Idaho.

into a huge jumble as they were moved out of the mountains and floated downstream. Lumberjacks in calked boots were stationed at the Sorting Gap, where jacks and booms were used to catch and separate the logs before entering the lake. Lumberjacks walked on the floating logs, and herded them together with pike poles according to their brands, then held them in place with boom sticks. From there, tug boats pulled the brails of logs to mills along the lakeshore for processing. The activity was promoted as an attraction by the Coeur d'Alene & Spokane Railway Co., which provided train and steamboat excursions for $2 to observe the stunning spectacle.

Damaged logs were caught in a boom and hauled across the lake to Shingle Bay, where homesteader Winifield Addington would saw and split the logs into four-foot lengths and sell them to steamboats for boiler fuel. At times there were as many as 1,800 cords of wood stacked along the shoreline to dry. (A cord measures 4x4x8').

Hn-dar-ep Scenic Wayside (Canoe Landing) Trail Miles: 10

WHERE AM I?
The southeastern bank of Lake Coeur d'Alene within the Coeur d'Alene Indian Reservation.

REST AREA AMENITIES:
Restroom/Accessible, Picnic Table, Interpretive Sign.
Next Stop: 2.1 miles

Sqwe'-mu'-lmkhw Scenic Wayside (A Familiar Place)
Trail Miles: 12.1

WHERE AM I?
The southeastern bank of Lake Coeur d'Alene within the Coeur d'Alene Indian Reservation.

REST AREA AMENITIES: Restroom/ Accessible, Picnic Table, Interpretive Sign.
Next Stop: 2.9 miles

Point of Interest: Before the days of Alottment, the Schitsu'Umsh spent the winters gathered in family villages along the lakes and rivers. Their fires crackled in long lodges made of wood, earth, and woven mats. The women wove mats and baskets from rushes, willow and cedar, repaired clothing, and made fur robes from marmot, beaver, coyote and lynx. This is where the men recounted hunting escapades of the previous season and repeated ancient stories about Grizzly Bear, Badger, and Coyote.

During spring, summer, and fall, the families dispersed to favored areas for hunting, fishing, and gathering. They picked berries in the mountains and dug for bitterroot and camas in the flatlands. They often met up with Spokane, Kalispel and Nez Perce for digging, trade, and ceremonies, and to make preparations for hunting parties.

Water potatos that grow in the mud along the lakeshore were the last food to be collected in fall. The women set up winter camps and gathered potatoes as they waited for the men to return from hunting in the mountains.

Point of Interest: As you approach Harrison you will encounter many fruit trees planted by early settlers along the hill side of the trail. Homesteaders planted and grafted fruit trees wherever they settled all around the area.

Looking south from the trail on the seven-mile portion that hugs Lake Coeur d'Alene

Steamboat Landing Scenic Wayside   Trail Miles: 15

WHERE AM I?
The southeastern bank of Lake Coeur d'Alene, within Harrison city limits, in Kootenai County.

REST AREA AMENITIES:
Interpretive Sign.
Next Stop: .3 mile

Point of Interest: Steamboats and trains met here starting in 1890, and this spot became a busy transportation hub. Pete the Greek's restaurant was over the water, and Pete Lang's Confectionary was built on stilts above the train depot. There was an ice house next to that, where ice was cut from the lake in winter and stored. The stately Hotel Harrison stood on the hill and a wooden boardwalk led up to it. Jim Patrou sold apples and oranges to passengers from a wheeled cart, and "Brown Sugar" Smith would meet the trains and carry freight and the mail up to people in town.

Interpretive sign at the site of Harrison's former steamboat landing and train depot

The first sternwheeler on Lake Coeur d'Alene was the Amelia Wheaton, built for Fort Sherman in 1878 to haul supplies to the fort and quell an expected Indian uprising that never materialized. During the gold rush to the Coeur d'Alene mountains in 1883-'84, the Army allowed prospectors headed for the gold fields to ride their boat up the Coeur d'Alene River to Cataldo.

Soon steamers such as the Boneta, Flyer, Georgie Oakes, Spokane, Colfax, and the Idaho traveled constantly between Coeur d'Alene, St. Joe City, St. Maries, Harrison, and Cataldo. Steamboats laden with people and supplies came down the rivers carrying lumberjacks whose leather pouches were bulging with money, and settlers crammed the decks with loads of hay, strawberries, vegetables, cedar shakes, and cordwood to sell at bustling markets in Coeur d'Alene. Indians rode the steamers free. They would wait along the riverbanks on horseback for the boats to pull up, then gangplanks were lowered so they and their mounts could board.

More than forty large steamboats plied the lake by 1910. They met the Inland Empire Electric Line railroad at Coeur d'Alene, which brought passengers from Spokane several times a day. Sunday excursions to St. Joe City were quite popular among the well-dressed travelers, even though that city was known as one of the wickedest settlements in the territory.

Trail Miles: 15.3 # Harrison Marina Trailhead

DRIVING DIRECTIONS: Take I-90 Wolf Lodge Bay/Harrison Exit #22 south 28 miles on the Lake Coeur d'Alene Scenic Byway (Hwy. 97). Turn right on the south end of Harrison's city park, go down the hill one block and turn left. Please park at the "trail parking" signs. The lower lot on the lake level is for marina customers and campers. However, if handicapped, you may use the ADA spot at the bottom of the hill by the public beach.

TRAILHEAD AMENITIES: Restroom/ Accessible, Picnic Area, Trail Information, Camping, Swimming, (Water, Food, Lodging, Shopping, Museum, Rentals, Laundry, Post Office nearby). **Next Stop: 1.3 miles**

The quaint resort town of Harrison is a favorite stop on the lake for cyclists, campers, and boaters.

ELEVATION: 2,150 FT. **Harrison, Idaho**

Many cyclists choose picturesque Harrison, Idaho, (pop. 210) as a base from which to explore the trail. There is **RV and tent camping** next to the trailhead on the lake. Go for a dip at the sandy **public beach** along the trail. The vault **toilet** across from the beach is open year round. Day visitors may use the coin-operated **shower** in the campground, where you can get a quick warm shower for six quarters. One of three popular marinas on the south end of the lake is here in Harrison, so boaters flock here for food, spirits, and dancing on hot summer nights. The city campground is centrally located in the midst of the action so don't expect it to be a quiet spot on weekend evenings. See **southlake cda.com** for listings of **live music acts**, lodging links, and events around the south end of Lake Coeur d'Alene.

The Trail of the Coeur d'Alenes (lower left) goes by the city beach and marina

Stay in
Harrison, Idaho *"Where the Trail Meets the Lake"*

Enter to Win
Getaway in Harrison
Details at harrisonidaho.org

Barn Dance
Saturday, May 7, 2016, Old School Gym

Live Music in the Park
Saturday Afternoons in Summer

Pig in the Park
Harrison Craft & Trade Fair
Saturday, June 11, 2016, City Park

4th of July
Fireworks on the Lake
Downtown Harrison

Haul Ass to Harrison
Annual Classic Car Show
September 10, 2016, Dowtown & City Park

Oktoberfest
Saturday, October 1, 2016, in the City Park

Winterfest
Saturday, December 3, 2016
Downtown Harrison

Harrison Idaho
Chamber of Commerce
www.harrisonidaho.org

VisitNorthIdaho.com

IDAHO
visitidaho.org

Harrison, Idaho

Harrison is all about fun on the water and **Harrison Pontoons & Rentals** specializes in getting you there with top-of-the-line equipment **rentals**. Up to sixteen people can enjoy the 24-foot Performance JC Tritoons, which, unlike most **pontoon boats**, go fast enough to pull **skiis and tubes**. Another option is the Sea-Doo Speedster. It's a cross between a jet ski and jet boat and pulls tubes and skis. You can also rent a Bass Tracker or smaller aluminum **fishing boat** from this local family-owned business.

The Reinhardt family also offers comfy **vacation homes** in the area, so check out the package deals online at harrison pontoons.com, or call 208. 696.1770.

Harrison Pontoons & Rentals offers a variety of boats, water toys, and package deals with vacation rentals on the lake.

Famous **One Shot Charlie's** café and bar is up the hill from the trailhead in the historic brick building that once housed the International Order of Oddfellows. Just about anywhere you go in the Inland Northwest, you run into folks who have partied at One Shots. During summer, the bar and cafe' are open seven days a week for lunch and dinner. The bar features fun creative cocktails and rotating craft and domestic draft handles. The café serves pizza, sandwiches, burgers, fresh salads and lasagna. Outdoor seating overlooks the park and marina. **Live music** and special theme parties happen year round and are posted on One Shot Charlie's facebook page. They stay open year round.

The Tin Cup is up the hill on the corner of the building's second level. They serve organic free trade coffee drinks and a limited breakfast selection of quiche, baked goods, oatmeal, fresh fruit, and yogurt. Open five days a week, between 7 a.m. and 2 p.m. in summer, they are closed Thursday and Friday. The Tin Cup accepts orders for "take-n-bake" quiches, pot pies, and fruit pies. Ask what they have on hand or what they're willing to make on custom order. 208.689.3088. They take a vacation in winter and reopen for the season in spring.

Also, on the second level find **O'Susanna's Design Studio**, a salon and gallery, where in addition to hair styling services, Susan carries beach dresses and sells jewelry and glass art creations she makes. The **Gallery at Harrison** above One Shot Charlie's is a favorite stop for

Harrison, Idaho

lovers of **arts and crafts**. They are open May through end of September. **Grubby Girls Soap shop** showcases handmade soaps and skin care products.

The Landing, a half block south, features an elegant breakfast menu that includes an orgnic *chicken fried chicken,* and for lunch and dinner they serve pasta dishes, seafood, steaks, seasonal salads, sandwiches, and housemade sauces with quality ingredients. Enjoy classic cocktails, Northwest wines, and craft drafts on the deck while watching a spectacular Harrison sunset over the lake. They are open seasonally, with weekend hours in spring, and ramp up to full hours as the weather warms.

The Harrison Creamery & Fudge Factory is one door south of The Landing in the building that once housed Harrison's first bank. People line up here for ice cream all summer long.

For the past few years, people who Harrison during the quiet stretch between October and May have faced a challenge when it comes to finding breakfast, especially on week days. Inquire about breakfast when making reservations and plan accordingly. The Osprey Inn B&B is open year round and breakfast is the owners' favorite meal, so you're in good shape there. An alternative is to rent a kitchen suite at the Lakeview Lodge and bring food. The Trading Post grocery store opens at 9 a.m. in winter and offers hot case breakfast sandwiches and coffee.

The city's oldest building is **Crane House Museum,** across from the Tin Cup. See Harrison's artifacts there and ponder its glory days as the former largest city in Kootenai County. Browse the old city jail, model steamboats, antique furnishings, and logging and milling machinery. The museum has old photos, local history books, and a collection of **local oral histories** for sale on CD. The volunteer-run museum opens weekends for the summer after Memorial Day, from noon to 4 p.m. Admission is free, but donations are appreciated.

Point of Interest: A branch of the O.R. & N. Railroad reached Harrison in 1890 and a thriving town sprag up from a squatters' settlement on the Indian reservation. Silas Crane arrived in 1891 and built the town's first house, followed by a general store the following year. Running water, electricity, and telephone service were estabished by 1902. Sawmills and box factories soon lined the waterfront and millions of board feet of timber were stored in the lake awaiting milling. The city directory of 1911 recorded a population of 1,250. At the time, Harrison had a bank, opera house, drugstores, grocery stores; hardware, furniture,

Harrison, Idaho

clothing and jewelry shops, a tailor, blacksmith, barber, shoemaker, bakery, churches, hospital, restuaurants, and hotels.

Adults had a different attitude toward child rearing in those days. Typical values of the era were evident in Harrison, where frontier life was tough, everyone worked hard to survive, and children were treasured but not coddled. Things that would be considered child abuse today are recalled with fondness and pride by the old timers. For example, one resident observed two young boys constantly fist fighting on the street. Rather than try to break it up, like most adults would do these days, he bought them both a set of boxing gloves to make the contest more interesting.

Andy Knutsen had a paper route by the time he was eight. Every day after school he would fetch a bundle of papers from the afternoon train and distribute them around town. In winter, when the temperature dipped below zero and the snow was knee deep, he beat back the darkness by wearing a miner's helmet with a carbide light that shot a flame out ahead of him. "It made me feel grown up to go through the miserable weather at night," he recalled. Most of the $5 a month he earned was spent at Pete's Confectionary on candy, ice cream, and soft drinks. Boys as young as seven worked as nailers at the box factory after school and on Saturdays. Some of the older boys could nail a hundred egg case box ends in an hour to earn about $3 during an eight hour shift. It was not unusual for boys of nine to find full-time summer employment at the lakefront mills and factories.

But life wasn't all school and work for Harrison's little ones. They climbed Sala's cliff on the east end of town and entertained themselves with whatever scraps and disgards they could find. On a trip to town, one might encounter youngsters chasing one another while balanced on six foot stilts, playing pranks, or selling bouquets of wildflowers to earn nickels for candies at the confectionary. Nearly a thousand travelers came through town daily, so there were plenty of potential customers. Steamboat passengers amused themselves by tossing dimes into the water to watch kids dive for them off the docks.

It was not unusual for children to swim a mile across the lake and back. Timing was everything, with the forty steamboats on the lake and tugs pulling long brails of logs behind them.

Harrison, Idaho

Point of Interest: The people of Harrison relied on wood and steam for heat and power, so fires often broke out and threatened the structures and sidewalks made from lumber. A devastating inferno in 1917 destroyed most of the town. The flames started at the Grant Mill, where the marina is now. The fire raced uphill and burned all the businesses that stood where the Harrison City Park is today. The rubble remained for more than thirty years until a park was finally established.

Today, Harrison's City Park is flocked by big shade trees and colorful flowers. It overlooks the trailhead and lake, and many cyclists rest in the grass here. There is free live music Saturday afternoons during summer. The band lineup is at harrisonidaho.org/entertainment. **Restrooms** with flush toilets are open seasonally. Find out more about Harrison's buildings and former waterfront mills and factories by picking up the self-guided **Historical Walking Tour Map** at the Crane House Museum or participating businesses. All the buildings around the park are on the National Register of Historic Places. See details and photos online at harrisonidaho.org/history.

Look for the outdoor **Grange Market** in the pocket park between the Harrison Grange and **Public Library** on Saturdays, starting at 10 a.m. through the summer. Country Fair in the Marler Brass building next to the Grange has resort wear like bathings suits and sunglasses. The **post office** is next door in the Corskie Building.

Harrison Trading Post, on the corner, is a combination grocery store, deli, bakery, and liquor store. They have coffee, breakfast sandwiches, and fresh baked pastries in the morning. The deli section has sandwiches made to order, prepared salads, hot case items and frozen yogurt with toppings. There is a new **camping** section with

Harrison, Idaho

basics like stoves, tents, super bright headlamps, and propane cannisters. The next food and water are 25-miles away at Cataldo, so stock up here before leaving Harrison.

The former Pedal Pushers Bike Shop, across from the Trading Post, is now **Cycle Haus Bikes & Brews**. The new owners are Teri and Rusty Riberich, who started HI Water Adventures in Harrison ten years ago. A building has been added for bike storage, display, and repair, which created a grassy courtyard area for relaxation, as well as more space in the original shop for a full service espresso bar and lounge. The rental bike selection includes comfort, hybrid, mountain, and road bikes, along with tandems, recumbents, children's bikes, and trailers.

Next door is **Sheppard Fruit Wines' tasting room** where delicious wines crafted on Harrison Flats by Jim and Julie Sheppard can be sampled and purchased. The selection for 2016 is: elderberry, cranberry, raspberry, rhubarb, huckleberry, and pear. Wine can now be purchased by the glass and enjoyed in the new pergola. Occasionally they will offer hors d'oeuvres and host barbecues. They suggest that you like their facebook page to stay informed about upcoming events. The tasting room is open noon to 5 p.m. daily during summer. Mention this guidebook to receive a **5% discount** on your purchase.

Harrison, Idaho

The Bird's Nest across the street in the Grant Building is a popular shop for lodge and cabin décor, and garden art with themes that express the Northwest lifestyle. Souvenirs with lake and **cycle themes**, and moose, bear, deer, birds, and other outdoor designs, decorate cups, shirts, bags, treats, and customized signs. Find comical greeting cards, retro **postcards** and more here. The Bird's nest is open daily July through mid-October, with seasonal hours in autumn and spring. Ower Shelly offers Christmas items during Winterfest. After that, she may open by special request when she's around, so give her a call.

The Company Store in the historic Grant Building is filled with antique, vintage and upcycled wares, and architectural salvage. The building originally served as a general store with a meeting hall upstairs for Harrison's Freemasons. Browsing the Company Store has

Harrison, Idaho

become a popular visitors' pastime as the wares spark conversations about memories and stories of bygone times. The constantly revolving collection includes items from historic Harrison, the Silver Valley, Spokane, and Seattle, including both antique and newly handcrafted furniture, gently used boutique clothing, art, tools, glass, Pyrex, vinyl, vintage fixtures, trinkets, and old books that people carry out by the armload. Some shoppers haul their treasures home by boat. (Cyclists may inquire about shipping). The store is open daily in summer from about 10 a.m. to 6 p.m., and sometimes later. In fall and winter, hours are generally Thursday through Sunday, noon to 5 p.m. If you are visiting Harrison during the slow season, somebody is usually around to come and open the doors. Make these arrangements by calling or texting Paul Hoskinson, 208.699.2228.

The **Laundromat** has reopenned. It is on the basement level, across from the pubic restrooms at the park. It is open 24 hours a day.

Lakeview Lodge, is one block further northeast. Every unit has a private balcony and unobstructed lake view. Each room is uniquely decorated in cabin style. All have air-conditioning, free **Internet**, complimentary coffee, refrigerators, and microwaves. Some suites have **kitchenettes** stocked with everything required for an extended stay. Just bring the food. Guests have free use of the barbecue. The lodge is a favorite among cyclists, who gather on the patio to sip their favorite beverages and share trail tales with other riders. You may lock cycles to the railing, or request secure bicycle storage. The public beach, park, restaurants, bars and trail are all within short walking distance of the lodge. Guests may park vehicles here free while continuing to explore the local recreational trails. Lakeview Lodge is open all year with special rates during the quiet season.

Harrison, Idaho

CORSKIE HOUSE B&B is next to the motel. Another popular stopover for cyclists, this historic house was built by Idaho's first known pharmacist after the 1917 fire destroyed his original home. The immaculate inn overlooks the lake and trail. It has four bedrooms with private baths, **Wifi**, and a den with a **pool table**. Relax on the back porch and enjoy the greenery and view of Lake Coeur

d'Alene. There is secure cycle storage on site and owner, Russ Wilbur, serves a **hearty breakfast** to get you on the trail in the morning.

For the **Osprey Inn Bed & Breakfast**, ride two blocks northeast on Hwy 97. This boutique B&B in a historical building has five vintage hotel rooms decorated with antiques. Each has a private bath with shower. There is free Wifi and a common room to watch TV and movies. Owners, Larry and Sherry, share their love of breakfast by offering three options: a continental breakfast for early birds, a three-course meal at 9 a.m., or a boxed breakfast to go. There is secure storage for cycles. See details at ospreybnb.com. The building was originally a boarding house for the Export Mill workers and served as a hospital for a short time.

The Thompson Lake Wildlife Management Area is on the north end of town. It can be reached on the trail by riding to Springston and going over the wooden plank bridge to the lake.

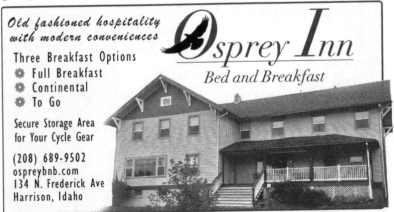

Anderson Lake Scenic Wayside

Trail Miles: 16.6

WHERE AM I?
The south side of the Coeur d'Alene River, Kootenai County.

REST AREA AMENITIES: Picnic Table, Interpretive Sign.
Next Stop: 1.8 miles

Springston Trailhead

Trail Miles: 18.4

DRIVING DIRECTIONS: Take I-90 to Wolf Lodge Bay/Harrison Exit #22 and drive south 26 miles along (Hwy 97), Lake Coeur d'Alene Scenic Byway. Turn left onto Blue Lake Rd. before the bridge and drive 1.8 miles. Trailhead is over the wooden plank bridge.

TRAILHEAD AMENITIES: Restroom/Accessible, Picnic Table, Trail Info, 13 Parking Spaces/1 ADA.
Next Stop: 1.2 miles

Springston Trailhead on the Coeur d'Alene River

Point of Interest: Springston was a company town for the Russell & Pugh lumber mill. It had a railroad depot, the agent's home, company store, boarding house, post office, saloon, school, and at least 14 homes. People from upriver communities and the surrounding hills came down to shop at the store, which stood close to where the restrooms are now. The remains of the tugboat *Golden Star* lie near the bridge. By taking the dirt road opposite the bridge (southeast) you can access several undeveloped swimming areas at pullouts along a mile-long stretch of Anderson Lake.

Cottonwood Scenic Wayside

Trail Miles: 19.6

WHERE AM I?
The south bank of the Coeur d'Alene River in Kootenai County. Thompson Lake is to the north.

REST AREA AMENITIES: Picnic Table, Interpretive Sign.
Next Stop: 1.1 miles

Gray's Meadow Scenic Wayside

Trail Miles: 20.7

WHERE AM I?
The south bank of the Coeur d'Alene River in Kootenai County.

REST AREA AMENITIES: Picnic Table, Interpretive Sign.
Next Stop: 3.5 miles

Cave Lake Scenic Wayside

Trail Miles: 24.2

WHERE AM I?
The south bank of the Coeur d'Alene River between Swan Lake and Cave Lake in Kootenai County.

REST AREA AMENITIES: Restroom/Accessible, Picnic Table, Interpretive Sign. **Next Stop: 1.6 miles**

Point of Interest: You are riding through the 22-mile long Coeur D'Alene River Wildlife Management Area. Canada Goose, Yellow Warbler, Black Tern, Violet-Green Swallow; and Grebe are among 280 bird species that find habitat in the river basin. Nesting osprey build huge nests on the utility poles. If you are interested in learning more about birds along the trail and in the wildlife area, see the resource page at harrisonidaho.org/bird-watching.html. You will find links such as: Audubon checklist of birds along the Trail of the Coeur d'Alenes, a Fish and Game map of Thompson Lake Wildlife Refuge, and other links to the Idaho birding scene. Cell phone service will be spotty between here and Cataldo.

Medimont Trailhead

Trail Miles: 25.8

Medimont Trailhead

DRIVING DIRECTIONS: Take I-90 to the Rose Lake Exit #34. Travel south on the White Pine Scenic Byway (SR-3) for 12.2 miles to the Medimont turnoff. Turn right and drive 1.5 miles to the trailhead.

TRAILHEAD AMENITIES: Restroom/Accessible, Picnic Area, Trail Info, 12 Parking Spaces/1 ADA.
Next Stop: 3.8 miles

Lane Scenic Wayside

Trail Miles: 29.6

WHERE AM I?
Between the south bank of the Coeur d'Alene River and SR-3 in Kootenai County.

REST AREA AMENITIES: Restroom/Accessible, Picnic Table, Interpretive Sign.
Next Stop: 1.6 miles

Point of Interest: This area has experienced devastating floods, like the one in 1933 that washed bridges from their foundations and swept them downstream. In response, the Army Core of Engineers presented a plan to build a 140-foot high dam at Springston that would have created a 34-mile long resevoir to provide flood control, irrigation water, and reserve water for power companies on the Spokane and Columbia rivers. The dam would have displaced four thousand small holders of productive farms and forests from Smelterville, Pinehurst, Cataldo, Kingston, Lane, Rose Lake, Medimont, Enaville, Black Lake, and Dudley. Twenty miles of their lifeline–the Union Pacific Railroad–would have been inundated as well. There were numerous public meetings where the landowners protested, but their projected losses were justified by the government because of the greater benefits the dam would supposedly bring to the region.

The government was not able to prevail against 59 Silver Valley mining comanies, however, who opposed the project because it threatened the local economy rather than help it. Their spokesman, Donald Callahan, said flood waters that would have come within two miles of Kellogg, could have leaked into existing mines along the Osburn Fault and curtailed potential underground exploration in the area west of Kellogg. The government finally abandoned the idea based on the realization that the $36 million cost of the dam was equal to about one year of revenue from the mines.

Trail Miles: 31.2   # Black Rock Trailhead

DRIVING DIRECTIONS: Take I-90 to the Rose Lake Exit #34 and travel south on SR-3 6.1 miles. Turn right after the bridge across the Coeur d'Alene River.

TRAILHEAD AMENITIES: Picnic Table, Interpretive Sign. 13 Parking Spaces, none marked ADA.
Next Stop: 2.3 miles

Trail Miles 33.5   # Bull Run Lake Trailhead

DRIVING DIRECTIONS: Take I-90 to Rose Lake Exit #34 and travel south on SR-3 3.2 miles to the community of Rose Lake where you will see a sign pointing to the trailhead. Turn left over the single-lane bridge, then right to the parking area.

TRAILHEAD AMENITIES: Restroom/ Accessible, Picnic Area, Trail Info, 10 Parking Spaces/1 ADA. **Next Stop: 1.4 miles**

Rose Lake, Idaho

Point of Interest: The settlement at Rose Lake sprang up around the Winton Lumber Co. mill along the railroad near Bull Run Trailhead. Some 900 people lived at Rose Lake until the Great Depression, when the mill shut down. There was a general store, ice cream parlor, barber, butcher, and boarding house for single men. The company built a large YMCA with tennis courts, bowling alley, and library. Silent movies accompanied by a pianist were shown weekly.

Watson's Rose Lake Resort is two miles from Bull Run Trailhead, Take SR-3 north 1.6 miles, then turn west on Watson Rd. The resort is .5 mile farther at the end of the road. Courtesy shuttles are not being offered this year. Overnight visitors can rent the vacation suite, cozy camping cabin, or pitch a tent in the grass. The camping cabin is fully furnished with bed, fridge, microwave, TV., and bowl and pitcher in lieu of running water. Water spigots and privvy are outside. The vacation suite is above a 100-year old tavern that is generally open only on Saturdays. Rooms can be rented separately, hotel style, with shared bath and full service kitchen. See pictures online. If you are traveling by cycle, bring food to last until you get to the Mission Inn restaurant in Cataldo, or plan to cycle another two miles north to the Rose Lake Restaurant (open daily 7 am to 3 pm). Please reserve online or message via the website contact form. Before the resort, you can turn off Watson Rd. to a public **campground** where there is a **restroom, picnic area**, and boat launch on Rose Lake.

Cedar Grove Scenic Wayside   Trail Miles: 34.9

WHERE AM I?
The south bank of the Coeur d'Alene River in Kootenai County.

REST AREA AMENITIES: Picnic Table, Interpretive Sign.
Next Stop: 1.5 miles

Rose Lake, Idaho

Trail Miles: 36.4 **Dudley Scenic Wayside**

WHERE AM I?
The south bank of the Coeur
d'Alene River in Kootenai County.

REST AREA AMENITIES: Picnic
Table, Interpretive Sign.
Next Stop: 2.2 miles

Trail Miles: 38.6 **River Bend Scenic Wayside**

WHERE AM I?
The south bank of the Coeur
d'Alene River in Kootenai County.

REST AREA AMENITIES: Restroom,
Picnic Table, Interpretive Sign.
Next Stop: 1.5 mile

Trail Miles 40.1 **Latour Creek Scenic Wayside**

WHERE AM I?
The mouth of Latour Creek on
the south bank of the Coeur
d'Alene River in Kootenai County.

REST AREA AMENITIES: Picnic
Table, Interpretive Sign.
Next Stop: 1.9 miles

Point of Interest: There was a small settlement at Dudley with a post office, store, and a grade school. Logs from the Winton railroad camp on Fourth of July pass were hauled down to Dudley by railroad and unloaded at the landing. Then they were towed down the river by steamboat to the Winton Mill at Rose Lake.

Kahnderosa Campground, .2 mile before the Cataldo Trailhead, has lots of room for **RV camping** and **tenting** along the river.

Winton Logging Co. lumber drive crew in a bateau near Cataldo, 1933. Photo courtesy Museum of North Idaho.

Cataldo Trailhead   Trail Miles: 42

DRIVING DIRECTIONS: Take 1-90 to Exit #40. Off ramps from both sides of I-90 lead to Latour Creek Rd. Turn right and drive to the stop sign. The trailhead is on the left within .2 mile or less, depending on the ramp used.

TRAILHEAD AMENITIES: Portable Toilet (removed after the peak season), Picnic Area, Trail Info, 10 Parking Spaces/1 ADA. (Bottled Water, Food, Camping, Post Office nearby). **Next Stop: 1.6 miles**

Cataldo, Idaho   ELEVATION: 2,140 FT.

This is the unincorporated town of Cataldo, 27 miles east of Coeur d'Alene, on the border of Kootenai and Shoshone counties. The **post office** is adjacent to the trailhead.

If you've pedaled from Harrison, you're probably ready for a good meal. Luckily, the award winning **Mission Inn Café & Grill** is across from the trailhead. The restaurant has received recognition for **best chef, steak, wine and beer selection,** and **best server/ bar tender** in the Silver Valley. For lunch or dinner, choose from among the fresh salads, or create your own from the salad bar. There is a large array of burgers and sandwiches, homemade soups, chili, steaks, prawns, oysters, cod, and salmon. Pair your meal with beer or wine from the huge selection, or have a shake. The healthy fish tacos made with poached cod with mango salsa and Louie Sauce, are a popular favorite. **Pulled pork** sandwiches and **barbecue ribs,** made with Ann's signature barbecue sauces are also a hit. (Purchase Anne's sauce to go by the pint or quart). Don't forget to leave room for pie.

Dine inside or under the beautiful trees outside. Free primitive camping is available. Catch up on your networking with the **free Wifi**. Local musicians may pop in for an impromptu jam session on Saturday night. Better get bottled **water** for the next leg of the journey.

Cataldo, Idaho

The Coeur d'Alene's Old Mission State Park is on the site of a traditional Coeur d'Alene tribal village. This Connecting Trip provides enriching historical perspective and cultural understanding of the land you are passing through. Idaho's oldest standing building, the Sacred Heart Mission, is here, along with a parish house, interpretive trails, visitor center, and gift shop. A modern museum on the grounds features the multimedia exhibit: *Sacred Encounters: Father DeSmet and the Indians of the Rocky Mountain West.*

The Old Mission was a spiritual center, wayside rest stop, and melting pot along the Mullan Road, where an eclectic mix of Indians, priests, soldiers, prospectors, entrepreneurs, and people of many nationalities found hospitality and shared stories on any given night. The mission was at the head of navigation for steamboats from Lake Coeur d'Alene, and it was a staging area for pack trains heading to the Eagle City gold mining camp. The Wyatt Earp family was among the throng that got off the Amelia Wheaton here and spent a cold winter's night in a tent before proceeding on horseback to Eagle City.

The park is an easy ride 3.5 miles west of Cataldo Trailhead. Turn left from the trailhead, cross the bridge over the Coeur d'Alene River, and travel west on Canyon Rd. for 2.2 miles. Go left on Dredge Rd. and proceed another mile to the I-90 overpass, then follow the sign. Summer hours are: 9 a.m. to 5 p.m., April through October. $5 per vehicle to enter park/$5 per person or $10 per family to enter the museum. Call 208.682.3814 for more information.

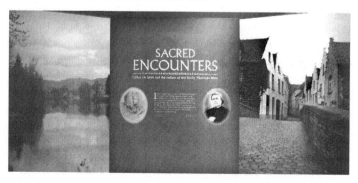

Pine Meadows Scenic Wayside
Trail Miles: 43.6

WHERE AM I?
The north bank of the Coeur d'Alene River in Shoshone County.

REST AREA AMENITIES:
Picnic Table.
Next Stop: .7 mile

Gap Rock Scenic Wayside
Trail Miles: 44.3

WHERE AM I?
The north bank of the Coeur d'Alene River in Shoshone County.

REST AREA AMENITIES:
Picnic Table, Interpretive Sign.
Next Stop: 1.2 miles

Backwater Bay Scenic Wayside
Trail Miles: 45.5

WHERE AM I?
The north bank of the Coeur d'Alene River in Shoshone County.

REST AREA AMENITIES:
Picnic Table, Interpretive Sign.
Next Stop: 1.6 miles

On the trial between Cataldo and Pine Meadows

Point of Interest: The Schitsu'Umsh tribal chief and prophet, Circling Raven, was buried near Kingston in 1760. He had foreseen the coming of the Black Robes and told his people about the Savior of the World. In 1740, Circling Raven and his group set up a winter camp in the vicinity of what is now Kingston—or *The King's Town*, after returning from a bison hunt on the Great Plains. A Coeur d'Alene tradition says the first Christmas was celebrated here by the Natives that year, a century before the first Jesuits arrived. It is assumed that French Canadian trappers had planted the seeds of Christianity among the Inland Northwest tribes.

Enaville Trailhead   Trail Miles: 47.1   ELEVATION: 2,224 FT.

DRIVING DIRECTIONS: From I-90 take Kingston Exit #43 and head north 1.2 miles up the Coeur d'Alene River Rd. The trailhead is on the left.

TRAILHEAD AMENITIES: Restroom/ Accessible, Picnic Table, Interpretive Sign, 10 Parking Spaces/1 ADA. (Food nearby).
Next Stop: 1.6 miles.

Kingston, Idaho (Enaville)

The north and south forks of the Coeur d'Alene River converge by the unincorporated town of Kingston, in Shoshone County. The trailhead overlooks a habitat rich with migratory songbirds and the interpretive sign helps you identify them by their singing styles.

Many cyclists have wined and dined at the **Enaville Resort,** a.k.a. The Snakepit. When former owners and avid trail supporters, Joe and Rose Mary Peak, passed away in 2012, the place closed, then changed hands. Now it is flourishing under new ownership with great food, live entertainment, rustic mountain atmosphere, and a Rocky Mountain Oyster Hall of Fame. Keep up with them on Facebook. Call 208.682.3453.

Point of Interest: When gold nuggets were found in Eagle Creek northeast of here, the news went viral and caused a stampede of some 5,000 hopeful prospectors and entrepreneurs to the Coeur d'Alene Mountains. Part of the frenzy was due to a Northern Pacific Railroad brochure that said any man with a pick ax and $77 could get a first class ticket from St. Paul, Minnesota, to Montana to try his hand at striking gold. After landing, most got outfitted at Thompson Falls, then came a 25-mile hike over the densly forested pass to Eagle City. There they found a rolicking tent city that sprang to life overnight and flashed in the pan for about a year. Others came by way of Spokane and crammed onto steamboats at Coeur d'Alene with their pack saddles and burros, sheet iron stoves, tents, shovels and picks, grub, and whiskey. They got off at Cataldo and continued to Prichard country over the Sky Trail by horse or on foot. Some hired swift water men who poled them up the North Fork. Most of this activity occured during the winter of 1893.

When the gold diggings played out, those that didn't scatter turned to logging in the Coeur d'Alenes for a living. Annual log drives became a common sight on the North Fork. Enaville boomed during construction of the Idaho Northern Railroad up the river. At one time, two thousand men lived in railroad labor camps that dotted the shores.

Upper Enaville was at McFee Gulch, a half mile north of the Enaville Resort, a.k.a., The Snakepit. By 1910 buildings included the Finn Worker's Lodge, six saloons where thirty prostitutes plied their trade, a grocery store, and post office. Most of Enaville was swept away by the flood of 1933. A vintage grocery store that once stood on the east side of the river played a role in the movie *Dante's Peak*. It was later floated across the river and added to Albert's Landing, which is shuttered and for sale.

The North Fork country offers national forest camping at both free and developed sites. Go north from the trail .5 mile and cross the wood plank bridge to take the Old River Road. It is a flat and scenic 4-mile ride along the North Fork of the Coeur d'Alene River to the Bumblebee turnoff. There is an ADA vault toilet. Turn left and ride on pavement for slightly more than a mile to free dispersed camping along the Little North Fork, or go 3 miles to the Bumblebee Forest Service campground.

But if you want to pamper yourself in a laid back and hospitable atmosphere go straight on the river road another 1.8 miles to **Country Lane Resort B&B.** This is an excellent place to stop and **eat,** relax, **fish, swim, float the river,** or hang out around a fire and do absosutely nothing. Everything you need to survive is right there. The roomy **B&B, vacation home** and **campground** have accommodated large groups of happy cyclists through the years. The B&B has king beds, indoor **hot tub,** washer/dryer, and **breakfast anytime** in the restaurant. The **restaurant** and **lounge** have a loyal following that returns for generous portions of certified Angus beef, fresh made soups, and garden salads; and you don't have to get dressed up for dinner.

Their riverside camping area has an outdoor bar and stage for live music events, grassy tent areas and RV spots with 50/30/20 amp power and water. RV sites near the restaurant have full hookups. Bathrooms and hot showers are on site. Check Country Lane Resort on facebook to see when they have live music and other events.

To drive there from I-90, take Exit #43 and follow the Coeur d'Alene River Rd. north 5.5 miles to Bumblebee turnoff. Turn right after the bridge to the Old River Rd. and go north 1.8 miles. Watch for elk herds along this stretch. Check in at the restaurant upon arrival. Call 208.682.2698 for information and reservations.

Trail Miles: 48.7 ## Pine Creek Trailhead

DRIVING DIRECTIONS: Take I-90 to the Pinehurst/Smelterville Exit #45. The trailhead is north on the Coeur d'Alene River.

TRAILHEAD AMENITIES: Picnic Table, Interpretive Sign, 15 Parking Spaces/ 1 ADA. (Food, Camping, Shopping, Showers, Laundry, Post Office nearby). **Next Stop: 2.4 miles**

ELEVATION: 2,224 FT. **Pinehurst, Idaho**

The City of Pinehurst, pop. 1,619, is on the south side of the Coeur d'Alene River in Shoshone County. Take the paved bike path south along Little Pine Creek, .4 mile to **Brewed Awakening** espresso stand at Heritage Park and **By The Way Campground** across N. Division St.

By the Way Campground is nestled against the hillside right off the trail. Cabin and camping options include a bunk-house style **camping cabin** with power, drinking water, microwave, coffee pot, and mini-fridge, (you provide the bedding), and another larger cabin with kitchenette, a half-bath, two full-sized beds, couches, and two TVs. The shower house and restroom are steps away. 13 **RV spaces** have water and electric. (No sewer hookups, but there is a dump station on site); seven tent sites, several with picnic tables and fire pits. Non-guests can **shower** for a small fee. Thirsty trail riders are welcome to stop by and fill water bottles here.

Rv & Tent Sites
Two Cabins
Shower House

BY THE WAY
CAMPGROUND
PINEHURST, ID

bythewaycampground.com
907 N. Division, Close to the Trail
208.682.3311

Shoshone County Park is one block past the campground. It's a peaceful place to picnic in the grass. Find **public restrooms** there. Call 208.753.5475 to check park hours. The **Laundromat** is across the street. **The Tall Pine** eatery is .5 mile south of the campground. Check them out for burgers, sandwiches, shakes and more. For **Barney's Harvest Foods** turn into the parking lot just past

Pinehurst, Idaho

the Tall Pine. They are a full service grocer and carry some locally grown produce in season. For the **post office**, turn right on Main.

Back on the trail, Before Smelterville, you will come to a **Walmart.** A ramp leads from the trail into the parking lot and a bike rack near the front entrance. Restrooms are ADA accessible. Three-tenths of a mile further east is the Silver Valley Office Coeur d'Alene Ranger Station for the Idaho National Forest. Check the outdoor rack for **visitor information** on everything from medicinal wildflowers to gold panning in the forest. Also see: fs.usda.gov/activity/ipnf/recreation.

Smelterville Trailhead   Trail Miles: 51.1

DRIVING DIRECTIONS: Take I-90 to exit #48 and turn south. Trailhead parking is on your left before the stop sign at Main St.

TRAILHEAD AMENITIES: Portable Toilet, Bench, 17 Parking Spaces/none marked ADA. No overnight parking. Food, Water. (Post Office nearby). **Next Stop: 2 miles**

Smelterville, Idaho
ELEVATION: 2,224 FT.

The City of Smelterville, pop. 621, is on the south side of I-90 in Shoshone County. If you began in Plummer, you have pedaled slightly more than fifty miles. Reward yourself at **The Espresso Barn.** It's right on the trail across from the mine car display at the city's entrance. The

folks at the Espresso Barn have been serving the Silver Valley for more than a decade and have many satisfied customers. The delicious peanut butter cup granita is a popular favorite. They also serve iced lattés, espresso shakes, Chai tea, Italian sodas, juice, muffins, bagels, biscotti, and cookies. They open early daily. If you are riding with a large group you may call in your order and tell them your estimated time of arrival.

Back on the trail there is a Dept. of Parks and Rec. shop with a water spigot .46 miles east of Smelterville where bottles can be refilled.

Trail Miles: 53.1 **Silver Mountain Trailhead**

DRIVING DIRECTIONS: Take I-90 Exit #49 to Bunker Ave./Silver Mountain. Turn south over the Coeur d'Alene River and go .4 mile to the large parking lot on your right, across from Gondola Village. There is no sign that marks this as a trail-head.

North America's Longest Gondola at Silver Mountain, Kellogg, Idaho

TRAILHEAD AMENITIES: Benches, Picnic Tables, BBQ Stands, Interpretive Signs. (Restroom, Water, Food, Lodging, Swimming, Shopping, Museum, Rentals nearby). The Gondola Village parking lot is indistinguishable from trailhead parking. There are no ADA designated parking spaces. RVs should park on the far end of the lot, away from the resort and gondola area. **Next Stop: .7 mile**

ELEVATION: 2,308 FT. **Kellogg, Idaho**

The City of Kellogg, pop. 2,117, lies along the Coeur d'Alene River in Shoshone County. The **indoor water park, skate park, gold mine tour**, and one of the Northwest's top **lift-served mountain bike parks** make it a natural stop for families exploring the trail with kids.

The nearest services are across the street from the trailhead in Gondola Village. Find public **restrooms** next to the gondola boarding station just past **Noah's restaurant**. Gondola Village has lodging a water park, several eateries, and a sporting good store. There is an **ATM** in the lodge lobby.

Point of Interest: You can't be in Kellogg long without hearing about how the town owes its existence to a jackass—or donkey, for those who prefer the more delicate term. (The perfectly correct word for the animal is simply *ass*—derived from the official *Equus Asinus*). An ass that carried Noah Kellogg's grubstake on a prospecting trip in 1884, is said to have stumbled upon an outcropping of galena near Milo Creek. Long story short, The Bunker Hill Company sprang into existence and silver and lead ore worth millions has been extracted from rich underground veins.

The township of Kellogg was organized in 1892 and for many years "Uncle Bunker" was a generous benefactor to the welfare of its citizens by providing both good-paying jobs and perks, like a YMCA, and major contributions for the ski hill (formerly the Jackass Bowl) built in 1968.

Kellogg, Idaho

There are several lodging choices close to the Silver Mountain Trailhead. **Guesthouse Inn and Suites** on the east edge has an **indoor pool**, hot tub, secure bicycle storage, and continental breakfast.

Take the path south from the trailhead to **Silver Ridge**, where condo suites beckon to travelers who like a bit of luxury with their cycling. See pictures and make reservations at kelloggvacationhomes.com.

Accommodations at the **Morning Star Lodge** in Gondola Village include **studios, suites**, and **rooftop hot tubs.** You can see virtual tours at silvermt.com under the lodging/floor plans link. Secure storage for cycle equipment is included with your room. The lodge is a 2014 Trip Advisor Certificate of Excellence Winner. Lodging guests have access to Silver Rapids, Idaho's largest **indoor waterpark**, which offers amenities for all ages, from the tiny tots Pollywog Pond, to the Trestles bar, where patrons can soak in a hot tub overlooking the waterpark and sip drinks while watching people surf and body board on the FlowRider® wave. Dining choices at **Noah's Canteen** include steaks, fish, pasta dishes, fresh seasonal vegetables, wraps, pizzas, sandwiches, and decadent desserts. See **online menu** at silvermt.com, under the *Amenities* link. The outdoor fireplaces are a nice touch, as are the anti-prohibition photos in the full service lounge.

Silver Mountain Sports in Gondola Village is a sales rental and repair shop with pavement **bikes**, trailers, and a new fleet of mountain bikes for use in the Silver Mountain Bike Park. Comfortable *Specialized* cycle rentals for the Trail of the Coeur d'Alenes come with a helmet. The **apparel and accessory** selection includes Dakine, Fox, Giro, Smith, Oakley, and The North Face.

MARK VIELLE PHOTOGRAPHY © 2014

Here is a convenient Connecting Trip that will make you a hero with the kids. Take a 20-minute ride on North America's **longest gondola** for a day of mountain top fun. Park your road bikes at Gondola Village, switch out for some **mountain bike** gear at Silver Mountain Sports, and spend a thrilling day at **Silver Mountain Bike Park**, named by riders among the best in the Northwest. Choose from more than 30 downhill trails, where seasoned riders appreciate the variety of super flowy single track, rough, technical fall-line trails and machine built, hand-tuned jump lines. Beginners can ease into it with a mix of single and double track trails in the "Chair 3 Zone" with access to a shorter portion of the mountain that has plenty of options for all ability levels.

Those who enjoy recreating at a mellower pace can take a **gondola ride** up to beautiful interpretive **nature trails**, visit the Mountain House Grill, play some disc golf, and pick **wild berries** in late summer. (Watch for bears because they like them too). Do the **Ride and Dine** on Fridays, from late June to August, for live music and a savory barbecue dinner with all the fixings in a mountaintop setting. The summertime gondola schedule starts in mid-June and runs through the first weekend of October. See details on the August **Brewfest** and other mountain activities at silvermt.com/Outdoor Adventures. Top off your Silver Mountain visit with a night at Morning Star Lodge and a day of play at Silver Rapids water park.

PHOTO COURTESY OF SILVER MT

Kellogg, Idaho

The bike trail runs east behind the Guesthouse Inn and cuts through the center of town between Historic Uptown Kellogg and the newer section along I-90. Exploring this section of the trail continues on the next page. Meanwhile, if you have a craving for **McDonalds** or **Subway**, head north on Bunker Ave. over I-90 to Cameron Ave. This is also the street to find authentic **Mexican dining**, and other restaurants, groceries, a drug and variety store, and more lodgings.

Turn right on Cameron to find **Silver Horn Motor Inn**, a locally-owned motel and adjoining restaurant. Don't be alarmed if large barking dogs greet you when arriving at the guest desk. The Silverhorn offers a **16-foot swim spa** and free **Wifi, DVD library**, and **laundry** facility. All rooms have air-conditioning, microwave, and mini-fridge. Bicycles are allowed in rooms. Coffee is in the lobby 24 hours a day. Call 1.800.437.6437 for reservations. The adjacent **Silver Spoon Restaurant**, a long time local favorite, has closed with no immediate plans to reopen.

Ride east for the Trail Motel, IGA grocery store, Humdinger hamburger stand, and variety/drug store at the intersection of Cameron and Hill St. The Trail Motel is dated, but clean, and rooms are only $45 plus tax. If you like browsing second hand stores, you can indulge your passion at Cattails right next door.

Casa de Oro at 120 W. Cameron has delicious **Mexican** lunch and dinner specialties. The friendly service, relaxing atmosphere, and the best of old Mexico's recipes, make this a popular spot among locals and visitors alike. If you've worked up an appetite on the trail, you will appreciate their huge selection of Mexican-style beef, pork, chicken, seafood, egg, and vegetarian dishes. For dessert, it's hard

Kellogg, Idaho

to choose between a creamy flan, apple burrito with caramel sauce and whipped cream, or deep fried ice cream.

Going south on Hill St. leads back to the trail. After the I-90 underpass, there will be a **Yoke's** grocery store on the right. On the next block, look for **Hill Street Depot** on River St. across from the city park. They specialize in meat dishes paired with **microbrews** from North Idaho Mountain Brewery in Wallace. Hill Street Depot has outdoor seating and **Wifi**. Check out the unique fence made with bombs at the veteran's memorial park across the street between the Depot and the trail.

Kellogg's **Historic Uptown** is straight up Hill Street, with shops, restaurants, and services, including the **post office, museum,** and **library**. This is where you will find **Dirty Ernie's bar, The Pizza Palace, Moose Creek Grill, Wahing Chinese Restaurant, Kellogg Vacation Homes** rentals, and the **skate park.** You could pedal past the ball field straight up Hill St. to McKinley, but it's much easier to take the short path from Silver Mountain Trailhead. It's also the easiest way to reach the **Staff House Museum** and The Ridge condos.

Ride west on the trail from Hill St. through the park, past the city pool and community garden. Back at Silver Mountain Trailhead, take the path that leads south to the **Shoshone County Mining & Smelting Museum** also known as the Staff House. A stop here will deepen your appreciation of the Silver Valley's rough and tumble mining history, its colorful char-

Path from the Trail of the Coeur d'Alenes to Shoshone County Mining & Smelting Museum, aka The Staff House Museum

acters, and the martial law that was instituted when mining disputes erupted in the 1890s. The building was originally constructed in 1906 as a residence for Bunker Hill Mine Manager, Stanley Easton. The gift shop selection includes history books by local authors and silver jewelry. They are open May through Sept., 10 a.m. to 6 p.m. closed Tues. 208.556.1592.

Ride east on McKinley Ave. past Hill St. and the ball park for resturants in Uptown Kellogg. Some people testify that the family-owned **Wah Hing**Chinese restaurant at 215 McKinley is the best place Chinese place in North Idaho.

Kellogg, Idaho

Point of Interest: If you have heard the Silver Valley is one of the richest silver mining districts in the world, you may be asking yourself where all the silver is, and why this neighborhood has many empty stores. The rich silver deposits are embedded in a nine mile-wide swath between Pinehurst and the Montana state line.

The ground beneath you is laced with hundreds of miles of interconnecting tunnels that reach 10,000 feet deep in some places—and there are hundreds of people working down there now. More than 1.2 billion troy ounces of silver have been blasted and hauled out of these mountains since old Kellogg's donkey stumbled on the galena outcropping.

Much of the silver is in demand for products like cell phones and solar panels. A little trickles back to the valley in the form of commemorative rounds produced at Sunshine Minting in Coeur d'Alene. You can get these collectors' medallions at gift shops along the trail.

So why the empty storefronts amidst all this wealth? For one thing, where there were once dozens of mines in the area, now there are only four. Many of today's miners commute from the Coeur d'Alene area and do their shopping closer to home. This, combined with strict environmental rules demanded by the EPA translate to higher costs of doing business that can strain the bottom line for businesses in the Valley.

Look for the **The Pizza Palace** under the clock tower on the corner of Main and McKinley for **pizzas, calzones, pasta dishes, pita pockets, salads** and **espresso**. The addition of beer and wine is anticipated at time of writing. This place has pizzas named for precious stones, like garnet (BBQ Chicken with mozzarella, onions, bacon, and cheddar), and sapphire (pepperoni with onion, mushrooms, olives, sausage, mozzarella, and pizza sauce). Order a custom pizza or dragon eggs (calzones) from any of the meats, veggies, and specialty toppings. Create your own salad too. Just circle the ingredients you want and they will build it. If you don't feel like going out after a long day on the trail, give them a call. D**elivery** is offered along the Trail of the Coeur d'Alenes between the Kingston Post Office and Harvest Foods in Wallace. They are open seven days a week and also have **free Wifi**. They open at 11 a.m. Closed Sun. and Mon.

Kellogg, Idaho

Access the connecting shops at **Main Street Market** from inside The Pizza Palace, where two floors of intriguing vintage, collectible, and secondhand items are displayed for sale. Don't miss the **waterfall** and **mine tunnel replica** in **Pappa's Barn** basement.

Point of Interest: The lobby in the **Kellogg Post Office** on Division and Portland, features a historic mural of Noah Kellogg and his donkey. The work by Fletcher Martin is one of six WPA murals in Idaho. His original submission depicted a wounded miner being carried on a stretcher. The townspeople protested, saying it would be too depressing to have to look at every time they had business in the post office. So, this more lighthearted theme was chosen instead.

Kellogg's finest dinner house is at the end of McKinley on Division. The **Moose Creek Grill** featres steaks, fresh seafood, pasta dishes with **handmade pastas**, and **vegetarian** options cooked to perfection. Feast on a mouth-watering char-broiled Angus prime rib-eye **steak** with garden **wild rice** or Parmesan-garlic mashed potatoes.

Owners, Joel and Betsy, take great pride in the sauces, and desserts **prepared from scratch**. They offer an extensive wine list and a variety of beers in the bottle and on tap from **Wallace Brewing Co.** Enjoy your meal on the veranda, or surrounded by the family-friendly country ambiance inside. See the **menu** at moose creekgrill. com. Reservations recommended but not required.

Kellogg has a small **skate park** on Main and Division. You can find a **public restroom** there as well. Several Kellogg Vacation Homes are in this residential neighborhood between the uptown business area and Wardner.

Home Sweet Home Base for a Rail-Trail Vacation

The Summit is one of the four cabins at the Hillside Cabins in Kellogg

Cabana with hot tub at The Villa. All Hillside Cabins have private outdoor hot tubs.

Kellogg Vacation Homes are a great lodging opportunity for people exploring the Trail of the Coeur d'Alenes. They feature well-appointed vacation rental homes that are clean and cozy with all the conveniences of home. In many cases you can rent an entire house for the cost of a motel room. These are some of Kellogg's classic older homes that have been remodeled and meticulously maintained. Here are some examples of KVH rentals within a mile of the trail.

A cluster of four homes is tucked against the mountainside a few blocks from historic uptown Kellogg at *Hillside Cabins.* They are near good restaurants, the library, post office, and skate park. All homes include full kitchens, gas fireplace, washer/dryer, stereo, VCR, wireless Internet, gas barbecue, and most have a dishwasher. Each has its own private **hot tub**. The Backwoods home also has a pool table. There is plenty of covered cycle parking. These homes start at an amazing $60 per night.

Mooster Lodge provides the best of both worlds. It's like a home in the country with plenty of space to enjoy the outdoors, yet only two blocks to shops and restaurants. This 3 bedroom, 2 bath home has all the modern conveniences. It also features an electric fireplace, cycle storage, covered deck and hot tub with a view.

Mooster Lodge

The Mill House

Bring the family to the charming **Mill House** with a white picket fence that says welcome to small town America. It is also in historic uptown Kellogg, just a half mile from the trail and ski hill. Like all the Kellogg Vacation Homes, the kitchen is stocked with everything you need except for groceries. Washer/dryer, gas fireplace, barbecue, VCR, Wifi, and private covered hot tub.

The **Lazy Bear** home sleeps nine and has all the amenities you need , including, 2.5 baths, washer/dryer, game room with bar and pool table, hot tub, and gas BBQ. This home is an easy, flat ride from the trail, near grocery stores and restaurants on Kellogg's north side.

Lazy Bear

If a condo is more your stye, consider a suite at Kellogg's **Alpine Village**, a half mile from the Silver Mountain trailhead. Sleep five in a modern suite with a view of the hills that surround Kellogg, Modern kitchen, gas fireplace, wireless Internet, TV in every room and DVD player with a great selection of complimentary movies. There is a community hot tub, pool table in the lobby, and lockers for your equipment. The Alpine has indoor parking and space to secure cycles.

Alpine Village

See images of all Kellogg Vacation Homes rentals in the Silver Valley at kelloggvacatoinhomes.com. Owner, Francine is also a real estate agent, so if you're looking to stay for a night or forever, give her a call at 800.435.2588 or visit the office in the historic **Kellogg-Wardner Depot** right on the Trail of the Coeur d'Alenes.

Kellogg Vacation Homes   **208-786-4261 / 800-435-2588**
kelloggvacationhomes.com 10 E Station Ave, Kellogg, ID 83837

To return to the trail from Historic Uptown Kellogg, ride downhill (north) on Division to the trail crossing. The trailhead is along the trail and in a parking lot about a half block west of the Silver Valley Chamber of Commerce visitor center and the old Kellogg-Wardner train depot. Stairs from the parking area lead to the historic uptown district.

Kellogg Depot Trailhead   Trail Miles: 53.8

Kellogg Depot Trailhead with Excelsior Cycle shop just beyond.

DRIVING DIRECTIONS: Take I-90 to Exit #51, Division St./Wardner. Go south on Division, cross the trail, and turn right across from the Depot after the bicycle sign. Trail parking is at the far end of the parking area.

TRAILHEAD AMENITIES: Trail Info Interpretive Sign, Bench. Parking/ none marked ADA. (Restroom, Water, Food, Lodging, Shopping, Rentals, Laundry, Post Office, Visitor Info nearby).
Next Stop: 1.4 miles

Find a public restroom and get answers to questions about the area in the old train depot building.

The Silvery Valley Chamber of Commerce Visitor Center and Kellogg Vacation Homes offices are in the old Kellogg-Wardner Depot along the Trail.

Kellogg, Idaho

EXCELSIOR CYCLE is right on the Trail of the Coeur d'Alenes, between the trailhead and Kellogg-Wardner Depot. Owners Mike and Debbie Domy have served the region's cycling community for more than two decades. They **sell, rent**, and expertly **service** a variety of **cycles**. Dedicated repeat customers come from as far as Spokane, Seattle, Portland, Canada, and beyond, to benefit from Mike's fair prices, technical knowledge, and skill. They are open year round and carry a wide selection of **gear**. The folks here are a great source of **information** about the local cycling scene.

Point of Interest: Excelsior Cycle is in a former train depot that was built sometime between 1909 and 1914. An earlier depot stood here when the mining district came under martial law in 1892. Four companies of Fourth Infrantry soldiers deployed from Fort Sherman detrained here and built a makeshift stockade, also known as "the bullpen," along the railroad tracks. Some 1,000 protesting labor union miners were rounded up and imprisoned there in harsh conditions.

Elizabeth Park Trailhead Trail Miles: 55.2

DRIVING DIRECTIONS: From I-90 take Division St./Warder Exit #51, north to Cameron. Turn east, drive 1.3 miles parallel to the freeway. (It turns into Silver Valley Rd.). See Crystal Gold Mine at MP 52. Turn right across from the RV park and go under I-90 overpass at Elizabeth Park Rd. Trailhead is on the left.

TRAILHEAD AMENITIES: Picnic Table, Interpretive Sign, 20 Parking Spaces/None Marked ADA. (Camping, Mine Tour, Gift Shop, nearby)
Next Stop: 2.2 miles

Take an underground tour of the **Crystal Gold Mine**, just a short pedal north of the trailhead. See shiny deposits of gold and silver in the mine walls. Get an hour of free gold panning (seasonal) with mine tour. Open 7-days a week, Feb. 14 to Dec. 31. Summer hours are 9 a.m. to 6 p.m. Adults $14/Kids $8.50. RV camping on site. 208.783.4653.

Shont Trailhead Trail Miles: 57.4

Memorial to fallen miners of the Sunshine Mine disaster

DRIVING DIRECTIONS: From I-90 take Big Creek Exit #54. The trailhead is south of the Interstate along the river.

TRAILHEAD AMENITIES: Picnic Table, Interpretive Sign. 20 Parking Spaces/1 ADA. Miner Memorial attraction.
Next Stop: 3 miles

Big Creek

Ride north under the freeway to the **Sunshine Mine Monument**. The hum of I-90 traffic drowns into the background at this solemn spot that honors ninety-one miners who lost their lives in a catastrophic accident at the Sunshine Mine in 1972.

As you shop at local grocery stores or relax in the restaurants, consider that many of the people you brush shoulders with, or their families and friends, have spent a hard life working underground. Most Silver Valley families lost friends and loved ones at the tragic Sunshine Mine accident and many women became widows.

Point of Interest: Booming silver prices prompted the incorporation of Sunshine Mining Co. in 1918. The company employed 450 local workers, and produced more than 400,000 ounces of silver each month. More than 360,000,000 ounces were produced in all.

Osburn, Idaho

Osburn's **Gene Day Park** is before the next trailhead. It has tennis and basketball courts, volleyball net, playground, **water** fountains, **picnic areas**, BBQ pits, and **public restrooms** with one ADA accessible. The park is open daily May 1 through Sept. 30, from 7 a.m. to 8 p.m.

Numerous streets cross the trail in Osburn, each one with a stop sign. If you're camping at **Blue Anchor RV Park**, turn left onto Yellowstone at the fifth stop sign, 1.2 miles after Gene Day Park. Look for the bridge on your right and a small city park. The Blue Anchor is across the street. Blue Anchor has **RV** and tent **camping, showers, laundry, visitor information**, and **Wifi**. 208.752.3443.

Trail Miles: 60.4 Osburn Trailhead

DRIVING DIRECTIONS: Take I-90 to Exit #57 and follow I-90 BL south to Mullan Ave. Turn left on Mullan and right on Sixth St. to the trailhead.

TRAILHEAD AMENITIES: Picnic Table, Interpretive Sign, 9 Parking Spaces/1 ADA. (Bottled Water, Food, Camping, Shopping, Post Office nearby). **Next Stop: 4.2 miles**

Osburn, Idaho Elevation 2,520 FT.

The City of Osburn, pop. 1,545, is on south side of I-90 in Shoshone County. Ride north one block on Sixth St. from the trailhead to access stores, banks, and other services on Mullan Ave. Turn right on Mullan and go one block to **Mom's Vintage Eatery,** which serves breakfast, lunch, and dinner daily from 8 a.m. to 8 p.m.

Stein's Market grocery store with deli is across the street. **Osburn Drug** next door carries clothing, fishing licenses, and sundries. Go the other way for **espresso** at **Capparelli's** on third. The **Laundromat** and **post office** are on the way. The Blue Anchor is a few more blocks west.

Ride 3.2 miles past the Osburn Trailhead to a stop sign where the trail crosses Silver Valley Rd. A mile farther look for a small sign that says **"Welcome to Wallace."**

Wallace, Idaho

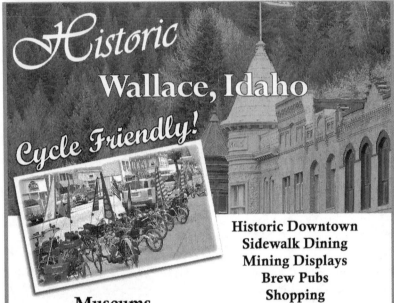

Wallace, Idaho

This statue at the Visitor Center Mining Exhibit expresses the relevance of mining to local families

Turn south and cycle under I-90 to access the Historic Wallace Chamber of Commerce **Visitor Center**. The visitor center is run by Chamber volunteers and is open daily during summer. Get free visitor information for Wallace and the region and view menus for the restaurants in town. Free coffee. The public restrooms are open year round, 24-hours a day. See the free outdoor **Mining Heritage Exhibit**. New outdoor signage tells the complete history and settlement of the Silver Valley, one of the world's richest mining districts. For information, call 208.753. 7151 during business hours, or visit the Chamber website at www.wallace idaho chamber.com.

The **Wallace Inn and Trailside Café** are one block east of the visitor center at 100 Front

Wallace, Idaho

The sky lights and large windows of the indoor pool at Wallace Inn provide an up close view of the mountains that surround Wallace.

Street, along the river. The Wallace Inn is rated an AAA 3 Diamond Property. Manager Rick Shaffer is the "Prime Minister" of both Historic Wallace and the Coeur d'Alene Trails, and he is dedicated to making sure you have an excellent stay. His primary objective is to ensure that cyclists visiting Historic Wallace have the most memorable adventure possible. So, feel free to call him at 208.752.1252 with all your questions.

Wallace Inn guests arriving by airplane may inquire about **shuttle service** from Spokane International Airport when making reservations. Guests that are cycling from another trailhead can arrange to be shuttled back to retrieve their vehicles. However, those who prefer to spend time in the **indoor pool, hot tub, steam room, dry sauna,** or **weight/exercise room** can ask to have their vehicles brought to the motel.

The shuttle van and trailer can accommodate up to 15 guests. Reserve it for a ride to Lookout Pass if you plan to ride the **Route of the Hiawatha.** Guests who want to rent equipment from **Excelsior Cycle** can request a ride to Kellogg as well. Wallace Inn has convenient and **secure indoor storage** for cycle equipment

Inquire about **recreational packages** with the Route of the Hiawatha, Silver Streak Zipline Tours, and White Water Rafting on the St. Joe and Clark Fork Rivers. See thewallaceinn.com for package details, or call 208.691.9169.

The Wallace Inn lobby, pool, and rooms are elegantly spacious. Rooms have king or queen beds, 32-inch flat screen TVs, mini-fridges, in-room coffee, hair dryers, irons, and free **Wifi**. There is a **pet-friendly** policy. You can purchase gifts and souvenirs in the lobby, like local history books, post cards, huckleberry chocolates and jams, silver and garnet jewelry, and **commemorative rail trail silver rounds**.

Enjoy the view through the adjoining four-season windows at the bright **Trailside Café** which is open 6:30 a.m. to 8 p.m. daily, with full room service until 8 p.m. Ask about the box lunches to take on the trail.

Wallace, Idaho

If you are staying at the **Hercules Inn,** leave the trail at the Visitor Center, and go one block past the Wallace Inn.

The Victorian Inn has spacious 500-sq. ft. suites with homey décor at an amazing price. They have firm king & queen beds, Direct TV on flat screens in both the bedroom and living room, **free WiFi**, and **laundry**. Cook on the **barbecue** or in the kitchen, which is fully stocked with everything but the groceries. Relax on one of the decks or in the outdoor **hot tub.** There is covered parking for cycles. Daily and weekly rates are offered. Call 208.556.0575 for reservations.

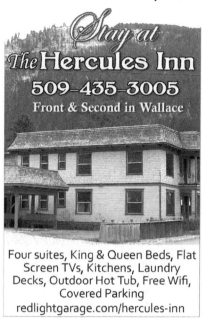
To get to the Historic Wallace 6th Street Trailhead ride north on Pine toward the Northern Pacific Depot Museum and turn left on Sixth, or return to the trail by the visitor center and ride .5 mile east.

You will want to turn north into the canyon for **City Limits Brew Pub and Wallace RV Park.**

Historic Wallace 6th St. Trailhead   Trail Miles: 64.6

DRIVING DIRECTIONS: Take I-90 to Exit #62, Wallace/Burke and take Bank St. to 6th St. Turn right and go past the Northern Pacific Depot Railroad Museum. Trailhead is on the right, over the bridge.

TRAILHEAD AMENITIES: Interpretive Sign, 6 Parking Spaces/2 Accessible. (Restroom, Water, Museum, at NP Depot Museum. Food, Lodging, Camping, Swimming, Shopping, Museums, Tours, Showers, Laundry, Post Office nearby).
Next Stop: 1.3 miles

Northern Pacific Depot Museum across the river from the trailhead is a visitor center with public restroom and drinking water

Wallace, Idaho   ELEVATION: 2,744 FT.

Wallace, Idaho, pop. 784, is the Shoshone County seat. The entire downtown is listed on the National Historic Register and the community has a great mix of historical architecture. It's easy to spend several days browsing, eating, and having fun in and around Wallace.

City Limits is the place to go for great food, craft beers, and camping. The menu ranges from Brewer's Scotch eggs to broasted chicken, and includes **vegetarian** and **gluten free** choices. See the menu at citylimits pubandgrill.com. Get a sampler of eight **North Idaho Mountain Brew** craft beers for $12. You can also get a 64-oz. refillable growler to go. The adjacent **Wallace RV Park** has 43 full hookups, **tent sites**, and three non-smoking **camping cabins** that accommodate from three to five guests. Bring your own sleeping pads and bedding. The bathroom/shower facility is **ADA accessible**. You can **shower** for a fee even if you are not camping. This is a **pet-friendly**, non-smoking establishment.

Northern Pacific Depot is a block south of the trailhead on Sixth St. You will find displays about the area's **railroad history, visitor information,** a **drinking fountain**, and **public restrooms**. Trains operated here from 1887 to 1992 and the museum commemorates the history of Wallace and railroading in the Coeur d'Alene Mining District. Shop for **souvenirs, T-shirts, locally-made items,** and **history books.** The museum is open daily May through October and hosts several events during the year, such as Depot Days in May and Under the Freeway Flea Market in September. The Depot is also available for private events, such as weddings. See npdepot.org for **cultural programs** and other scheduled events.

Wallace, Idaho

Point of Interest: Portions of the 1980 movie *Heaven's Gate* were filmed on this street and *Dante's Peak* (1996) was filmed all over town. The set construction for *Heaven's Gate* kept up to 100 laborers busy for several months as Sixth Street was transformed into a historical western town complete with dirt streets.

Albi's is under new ownership, remodeled, and smoke free with a new higher end menu. The current plan is to open for dinner from 5 to 9 p.m. on weekdays, posssibly until 10 p.m. on Friday and Saturday, but hours may expand.

Be part of the lively audience at **Sixth Street Melodrama** across the street from the museum. Cheering the heroes and jeering at the villains is part of the experience at the plays, many of which are original works inspired by local history and developed by people in the community. To see the show schedule and purchase tickets, go to sixthstreetmelodrama.com.

The **Silver Streak Zip Line Tours** welcome center is a half block west on Pine St. Zip line riders are transported from here up the mountain to three miles of cable on two courses. The western course has six runs, and the eastern course, four. Zip line rides are in high demand, so if you want to experience Idaho's biggest rush, review the policies about weight limits and health, make reservations, and pay in advance with a credit card at silverstreakziplinetours.com. If you drop in hoping for a spur of the moment ride, there may not be an opening.

If you are staying at the vintage **Stardust Motel**, keep going west on Pine, a half block past the spaceship on Fifth and Pine.

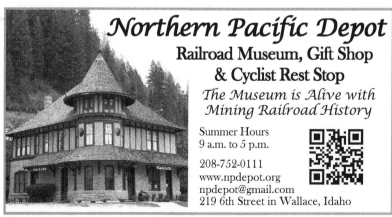

Wallace, Idaho

The Stardust Motel provides affordable vintage lodging in the heart of downtown Wallace. The spacious rooms include queen, and king bed options. All rooms have coffee makers, fridges, and **free Wifi**. If you desire a microwave, please request it when making your reservation. This is both a **pet-friendly** and cycle friendly establishment. Bicycles may be brought into rooms or locked to the railings. Guests are free to use the indoor **pool, hot tub, sauna, steamroom**, and **exercise room** at the Wallace Inn. If the Stardust office is closed when you arrive, check in at the Wallace Inn.

Point of Interest: Mrs. Lucy A. Wallace took a steamboat from Coeur d'Alene in the spring of 1885 to join her husband at the townsite he was establishing, called Placer Center at the time. She came prepared to set up housekeeping with a a dog, bird, cats, chickens, and all the necessary homemaking essentials. **Colonel W.R. Wallace** had located the town in the midst of a cedar swamp the previous year and people thought he was crazy. But he envisioned a prosperous mining center, which is exactly what Wallace became.

He greeted his wife at the Old Mission and they struggled through the mud by wagon and crossed the river 14 times. The water was high and dangerous because of the melting snow. The second ford crossed a narrow channel with a rapid current and their wagon became wedged between two boulders about midstream. Col. Wallace walked out on the tongue of the wagon with an ax and leapt to shore, where he cut some saplings and used them to pry the wheels free. A chicken drowned at another crossing when the wagon filled with water. By winter of that year, Mrs. Wallace was one of only four white women in the vicinity, braving the rigors of the mining camp lifestyle.

Wallace, Idaho

The Red Light Garage with spaceship on Fifth and Pine

Find tasty food, friendly service, and intriguing décor at the **Red Light Garage**, just steps east of the Stardust on Fifth St. They are known for their hearty breakfast burritos, espresso, **huckleberry pancakes**, and 12 varieties of delectble burgers, "the best along I-90." This year, owners Jamie and Barbara are adding a selection of 12 **specialty all-beef hot dogs** with a variety of toppings. **Vegetarians** can get a tasty meatless garden burger. Or, choose from wraps, salads, sandwiches, and shakes, of which huckleberry is a favorite. Dine inside or enjoy your meal on the patio. Customers like to climb into the spaceship—technically a Korean weather satellite—for a souvenir photo.

The following description of Wallace traces a route east from the Brooks Hotel on Fifth and Cedar then south on Sixth to Bank. The chef statue on the corner of Fifth and Cedar welcomes you to the **Brooks Hotel and Restaurant**. The restaurant and lounge are open daily for breakfast, lunch and dinner. They serve choice locally cut meats and potatoes grown in Idaho. Try a **huckleberry dessert** when berries are in season. They also sell locally picked **fresh berries** by the quart or gallon. If you would like a room call 208-556-1571 because the owners do not check their email very often.

Red Light Garage

Omelettes ~ Breakfast Burritos
"Best 24 Burgers on I-90"
Sandwiches and Wraps
New Orleans Muffuletta
Huckleberry Shakes

Inside/Outside Dining ~ Order to Go

OPEN DAILY 7 A.M. TO 7 P.M. IN SUMMER

302 5th in Wallace ~ 208-556-0575

Wallace, Idaho

The Metals Bar at 514 Cedar is open 10 a.m. to 2 a.m. daily. Relax and enjoy cold brews, local **Northwest wines**, or cocktails in this neighborhood lounge with a mining theme. You are likely to meet locals here who have worked in the mines and can identify each one of the locations in the **mine photos** on the walls. As you rub shoulders with folks born and raised here, you will find they are a wealth of information about the area. Play a game of **darts, pool,** or **shuffleboard.** Help yourself to popcorn or munch on dill pickle pretzels (kept in buckets under the popcorn machine). This is one of Idaho's many smoking bars. They installed a state-of-the-art ventilation system for non-smoking guests, and it is amazingly effective. They often have **live music** on weekends. See updates about The Metals Bar on their Facebook page.

Point of Interest: By 1892 dreams of glittering prosperity in the free wheeling Coeur d'Alenes were on hold. There were armed troops in the streets, women and children had been evacuated from Wallace, and miners were corralled in concentration camps called bull pens. What happened? It was the result of things going on in Washington, D.C. Congress had passed the Sherman Silver Purchase Act, a bill supported by pro-silver forces who wanted U.S. currency backed by silver as well as gold. After the act passed, the federal government started buying most of the silver produced in the U.S. The guaranteed market seemed like a godsend in the Coeur d'Alenes at first, but silver production went up as a result and soon there was a glut that caused prices to fall dramatically. By '82 mines were closed and the owners had proposed wage cuts. The union miners were working long hard hours by candlelight for $3.50 a day and refused to do it for less, so the owners brought in scabs. This spurred protests and violence that resulted in martial law.

The Metals Bar

Your full-service lounge
in the heart of
Historic Wallace

Happy Hour 4-6 pm daily

Mining History Display
Billiards & Darts
"Dill Pickle" Pretzels
Free Popcorn

514 Cedar St. in Wallace
208.752.5213

The first of a thousand troops detrained July 13, 1892: Infantry companies from Fort Missoula and Fort Sherman, and three companies of Idaho National Guard. There were 500 soldiers in Wardner, several companies in Burke, and more strung out between there and Wallace. They were ordered to shoot on sight any miner apprehended in the act of blowing up railroad bridges or mill property, no questions asked.

Wallace, Idaho

Rent a cycle at the newly opened **Fly Shop**, which specializes in fly fishing, but has a couple of 3-speed cycles at $20/day for tooling around. They come with a helmet and a lock. The custom wooden drift boat on display in the showroom is handcrfted by owner Gregg Maddock.

The Nook, across the street, is an intimate eatery that serves wraps, salads, and sandwiches on **fresh baked breads**. Everything is made from scratch. Open at 11 a.m. Mon. - Sat. The Nook delivers to the Wallace Inn, the Ryan, and The Banker. 208.556.5522. Next door you will find the **Sam Brooks Wallace Laundromat,** with the antique wringer washer outside, open daily from 7 a.m. to 8 p.m.

6th and Cedar is a café in the historic Wallace Corner building. They serve **specialty drinks** and **organic coffee** roasted locally at Silver Cup Coffee Roasters of Kellogg. New this year, a variety of seven types of bagles including: Veggie, California, BLT, Lobster with sun dried tomato, and Lox (Pacific smoked salmon) . They open daily at 7 a.m.

Point of Interest: This is the former **Red Light District** of Wallace. About a dozen brothels flanked the area around Sixth, Pine, and Cedar Streets for a century. Some bawdy (body) houses were registered as female boarding homes. Others operated out of Wild West saloons, dance halls, and burlesque theaters. The largest burlesque hall was called the Coliseum, located where the NP Depot Museum is now.

The Lux began operating on the northeast corner of Sixth and Cedar in 1977, one of a chain of brothels on the 600 block of Cedar–The Lux, The Oasis, The Luxette, and the U&I Rooms. Today **Lux Rooms** is a freshly renovated boutique hotel. The spacious Madame Suite includes private bath, mini-bar, fridge, and flat screen TV. The other rooms pro-

Window display at the Oasis Bordello Museum on Cedar St.

Wallace, Idaho

vide a retro lodging experience, which means no electronic contraptions except for the free Wifi. The main focus is the comfortable bed, and the birds eye view of downtown Wallace flanked by forested hills. Most rooms have their own sinks. Tubs/showers are down the hall. Ask about your options for secure cycle storage.

Rooms at the historic **Hotel Ryan** feature antique and vintage furnishings, free Wifi, and most have private baths. Most rooms have mini-fridges. Guests who desire a microwave need to request it when making reservations. Only the Owner's Suite has a TV. All rooms are accessed by stairs to the second level. The front door remains locked for privacy and security. The emphasis at both hotels is comfort and hospitality. Get your group together and rent an entire hotel. Call 208.753.6001 for details.

The **Silver Corner Bar & Grill** has been tastefuly revamped and is specializing in a variety of fresh hand-pressed burgers, along with several other options like fish and chips, chicken wap, and assorted sandwiches. They open for traditional American breakfasts, omelettes, and Belgian Waffles at 8 a.m., seven days a week.

Get a **guided tour** of Wallace's famous **Oasis Bordello Museum** across from the Ryan, for a glimpse of the everyday life of "working women" in this authentic brothel that closed in 1988. They open "around Memorial Day" to the end of September. Tours leave from the gift shop on the half hour. Admission $5. 208.753.0801.

Point of Interest: Barber George Bangart told the *Spokane Chronicle*

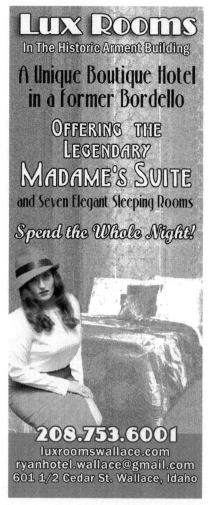

Wallace, Idaho

newspaper that, in his opinion, the Wallace brothels were a greater boost to the city's economy than the mines. He made this statement after the Lux and Luxette Hotel were temporarily shuttered for about a week in 1982. The region was in the midst of a mining slowdown, with more than half of Silver Valley's mines shut down and 34 percent of the workforce idle. To add to the city's economic woes, the brothels were closed after a traveling evangelist came to the local Assembly of God Church, preaching hellfire and brimstone, and comparing Wallace to Sodom and Gomorrah. Madame Delores Arnold calmed everyone down and smoothed things over in an undisclosed manner. "We had an understanding," she said, in a statement to the newspaper, adding, "Men need relief and they are well taken care of here." Stories of her contributions to the town are legendary and the Assemby of God church was one of her benefactors, as were the high school music department and the police department.

A new addition to Wallace this year is the **Friends of the Coeur d'Alene Trails Non-Profit Center** in the historic Pennaluna building at 413 Sixth St. There is a public restroom here and a place to refill water containers. The visitor center offers hospitality, cycle tips, information; along with men's and women's cycling jerseys and hats for sale. They are renting beautiful new 21-speed hybrid Marin cycles with lights, perfect for both the Trail of the Coeur d'Alenes and the RoH. There are also one-speed Deluxe cruisers with baskets and cup holders for leisurely tours around the area.

Friends of the Coeur d'Alene Trails has been instrumental in supporting and enhancing the local rail trails with improvements such as rest areas and signage. They have also mapped road rides throughout the area and posted directions on their website: friendsofcdatrails.com They publish and distribute thousands maps every year that show the entire Bitterroot Loop. Proceeds from the center will help the Friends continue with their activities, so drop in and check it out.

As you head south on Sixth St., you may feel yourself pulled by a mysterious force. That could be because you are approaching the **"Probablistic Center of the Universe,"** so dubbed by a former mayor of Wallace, as a challenge, more or less, to anyone who could disprove his assertion. When arriving at Sixth and Bank, you will see the **Center of the Universe** is a plaque at the intersection, that pays tribute to the central importance of mining in Idaho's Silver Valley, with stock symbols of the district's remaining mines decorating the perimeter.

Wallace, Idaho

The mouth-watering aroma wafting in the air comes from the smoker on the sidewalk outside the **Historic Smokehouse Barbecue & Salon,** on the corner of Sixth and Bank. The Memphis style barbecue can be enjoyed inside or at one of the sidewalk tables. Special diets are accommodated too, with daily vegetable specials and **organic** spring mix salad. Go to **smokehousebbqsaloon.com** to see the menu. Relax and absorb the good vibes of Wallace as you appreciate the ambiance of 1900s architecture framed against the hills that encircle the town.

Wallace District Mining Museum and Visitor Center at 509 Bank Street is open seven days a week in summer. Stop in to learn about the Coeur d'Alene Mining District's many contributions to this region and the world. There are scavenger hunts for the kids, and a twenty-minute film called, *Mining and the Center of the Universe.* See mine models and exhibits that give visitors a "true mining experience." There is a **public restroom** and **visitor information** about regional attractions.

Pay your respects to **The Last Stop Light** between Seattle and Boston, lying in state here. It hung at Seventh and Bank Streets when I-90 snaked through town. When highway expansion threatened demolition of the beautiful old buildings downtown, the citizens rescued Wallace by getting the entire business district listed on the National Register of Historic Places. The account of their success was written up in publications from coast to coast.

Wallace, Idaho

The museum gift shop has commemorative **silver medallions** and **books on local history**. Ask them about biking and hiking trails around Wallace, such as the **Pulaski Trail** on the outskirts of Wallace. Museum admission is $3 each or $7 per family. See wallacedistrictmining museum.org for special rates, events, and seasonal hours. 208.556.1592.

The **Sierra Silver Mine** waiting room is on the corner of Fifth and Bank. Board a trolley for a ride to an underground mine tour to learn about hard rock mining. Open daily 10 am to 4 pm Jun through August, and 10 am to 2 pm May and September. $15 adults/$8.50 kids. Tours leave every half hour.

The Banker is a charming vacation home across from the mine tour. It is in high demand but worth trying to secure because of its

quiet and rural feel while being right in the middle of all the downtown Wallace action. There is plenty of room for a family or group in this two-story home with three bedrooms, two bathrooms, living room with flat screen TV, Wifi, full kitchen with dishwasher, dining area, washer/dryer, and full basement for lots of secure cycle storage. Two night minimum stay starts at $125 with discounts for additional nights. See interior pictures at kelloggvacationhomes.com/banker.html and call 800.435.2588 for reservations.

Point of Interest: One of the West's last notorious dance halls passed into history when crusading moralists were able to force the closure of Wallace's Arcade Theater in 1911.

Wallace, Idaho

Step into some local history at the **Wallace Stairs** interpretive signs across from the 'Silver Mine tour, and **"Hike the Stairs"** for a bird's eye view of Wallace. Hiking all twelve of Wallace's historic stairways is the equivalent of climbing a 46-story building! See a quick tour of the stairs hike here: youtu.be/SR-QDiI_HCA.

Browse the unique **North Idaho Trading Co**. pawn shop at the junction of Fifth and Bank. This is also the home of the non-profit **Historical Wallace Preservation Society** which has catalogued and digized thousands of **pictures** of mining, logging, and railroading history in and around Wallace. Pictures can be purchased for a nominal fee.

The popular **Fainting Goat Wine Bar & Eatery** across from the mining museum has closed. Chef Rob, who formerly worked at the Goat, has opened a sandwich shop called **Blackboard Café** across the street in the space that previously housed Angie's at 517 1/2 Bank St. The decor is relaxing, and features a giant blackboard wall with hand drawn chalk art and inspirational quotes. There is a guitar hooked to a live amp for guests with musical talent to share an impromptu performance. New & classic sandwiches feature international flavors and an elegant flair at reasonable prices. The menu can be viewed online at black boardcafe.org, but selections are subject to change. They are open daily from 11 a.m. to 3 p.m. except Tuesdays.

Continue to the next block east on Bank St. for satisfying browsing at amazing antique and collectible shops. For example, the collection at **Wallace Antiques Gallery** is not to be missed if you love luscious old stuff. From the turquoise and silver jewelry to handmade furniture with a twist; antique toys, instruments, kitchen equipment, vintage seal skin boots, beaded items, old equipment, and surprises like the Radium Ore Revigator or the Cornetophone, it's all impressive. A video on YouTube by AuggieDog Productions accurately describes the place as a museum with price tags. You can get an excellent feel for what to expect at this, and Wallace's other antique shops, by viewing this video at: https://youtu.be/gcHNFfX7r84.

Wallace, Idaho

Leisurely sidewalk dining at the 1313 Club, the historical Heller building on Bank St.

The bike rack outside the **1313 Club Historic Saloon & Grill** says "Riders Welcome!" Get a delicious breakfast, lunch, or dinner at this cyclist-owned restaurant in one of Wallace's historic buildings. The Heller building has served as a hotel, bus depot, barbershop, and café. Decorations in this eclectic eatery include a nest of hibernating killer bees (safely tucked in a glass case), swooping piper cub, and a flying albino beaver.

Mexican dishes, steak, buffalo, big salads, homemade soups, wraps, and **vegetarian** garden burgers are some menu choices. The **huckleberry salmon** burger combines a homemade berry sauce and grilled onions over a salmon patty, for that quintessential Northwest flavor. Pasta lovers appreciate the "**Build a Pasta Bowl**." Choose spaghetti, penne, or fettucini, topped with one of three sauces: Alfredo, zesty meat, or marinara.

Enjoy the selection of **regional wines** and experience **microbrews** from **Wallace Brewing** while pondering the various theories of how the 1313 Club got its name. Try the award-winning Red Light Irish Red Ale, or the 1910 Black Lager, reminiscent of German dark beers, but without the bitterness. There is **free Wifi** here. Open 7 a.m., Mon. through Sat. Breakfast is served until 10:30 a.m. See the menu at 1313club.com.

To sample the rest of **Wallace Brewing's** eight local microbrews, step into the Orehouse tasting room next door. Tasting tarts at $1 per sample with larger servings available. Play free pool, chess, and hard

Wallace, Idaho

tipped darts. Inquire about a **tour** of the microbrew operation. You can stock up on brew by getting a growler-full for the road. 208.660.3430.

Recapture the refinement of days gone by at **The Silver Tea Room** inside **Price Tag Antiques**. Drop in for a pot of tea for one, or gather with new and old friends around an elegantly set table to enjoy a four-course luncheon tea, afternoon tea, or five-course full tea. Service is between 11 a.m. and 4 p.m. Please make reservations in advance for parties of three or more by calling 208.556.1500.

Price Tag Antiques is another must-see store for lovers of antiques and collectibles. There is a man cave for the guys this year, and a new boutique of vintage clothing on the upper level, with distinctive fashions from the past, furs and leathers, retro purses, and the best selection of hats around. The store has more than 7,000 square feet of quality Victorian, American, and European antiques, primitives, western items, and other treats. Note the original columns and tin stamped ceiling. Shelves on the east wall are vestiges of the Coeur d'Alene Hardware Co., incorporated in 1892. Summer hours are 10 a.m. to 6 p.m.

For the next stretch to Mullan, return to the bike trail near the NP Depot Museum on Sixth St., or you can catch the trail under the freeway across from **Harvest Foods**.

Restless Rapids Scenic Wayside

WHERE AM I? Trail Miles: 65.9
The South Fork Coeur d'Alene
River in eastern Shoshone
County.

REST STOP AMENITIES: Public
Restroom/Accessible, Picnic
Table, Interpretive Sign.
Next Stop: 1.8 miles

Golconda Scenic Wayside

WHERE AM I? Trail Miles: 67.7
The South Fork Coeur d'Alene
River in eastern Shoshone
County.

REST STOP AMENITIES: Picnic
Table, Interpretive Sign.
Next Stop: 3.7 miles.

Trail Miles: 71.4 **Mullan Trailhead**

DRIVING DIRECTIONS: Take
I-90 to Exit #68 to River St.
Trailhead is straight ahead.

TRAILHEAD AMENITIES:
Portable Toilet (seasonal), Pic-
nic Table, Interpretive Sign, 20
Parking Spaces/2 ADA. Room
for RVs. (Water, Food, Lodg-
ing, Camping, Museum,
Laundry, Post Office nearby)..
Next Stop: 7.1 miles.

Lucky Friday Mine Display, Mullan City Park

ELEVATION: 3,277 FT.   **Mullan, Idaho**

Congratulations! You have pedaled across the entire State of Idaho (granted, it was the skinny part), from one end of the Trail of the Coeur d'Alenes to the other. You are in the City of Mullan, pop. 692, in the eastern portion of Shoshone County, six miles from Lookout Pass Ski Area and the Montana border. The city park, two bloc ks up the street from the trailhead, is a pleasant place to relax in the shade.

Lookout Motel, opposite the trailhead, has tiny, clean, and **very low-cost rooms** with mini-fridges and TVs.

If you arrive during business hours, you can get visitor informa-tion questions answered at the city hall next to the John Mullan statue at Second and Earle.

Earle's Pub & Grub, formerly the Coyote Café, at Second and Earle is closed to business and for sale as of this writing. Chef Michael, who put out a lot of good food there is now at the Red Light Garage in Wallace. There is a **public laundry** with change machine and soap

Mullan, Idaho

dispenser in the building behind the lounge, and a clean **public restroom.**

The Silver Shaft restaurant, down the block closed shortly after the 2015 guide came out and has not reopened.

Across the street are the **city park**, **post office**, and **Captain John Mullan Museum**. The volunteer-run museum traces the history of Mullan with many artifacts donated by local families. See an old moonshine still and a detailed

The Captain John Mullan Museum opens weekdays in summer

model of the steamboat *Idaho*. Learn about the building of the Mullan Military Road. The historic newspapers are of interest to genealogical researchers, with a scanner and copy machine on site to aid the effort. Open weekdays, June through August, 10 a.m. to 4 p.m. or by appointment. Admission is by donation.

The **Outlaw Bar & Grill** across from the park on Hunter, is the only place left in town where a person can get a meal, as long as they are over 21. If you find the cigarette smoke problematic, the park has picnic tables in the shade. The Outlaw's menu is basic burger, chicken strip, fish and chips and patty melt. The chicken wrap is good, and so are the deep friend mushrooms.

Mullan House B&B at 501 Hunter has six beautifully decorated rooms with private baths, TVs, and Wifi. There is secure storage for bikes and a cleaning room. Guests have use of full kitchen and laundry. See more at mullanhouse.com.

Point of Interest: Hecla's FridayMine has been the predominate source of work in this valley for more than seventy years. It's impact on life in Mullan was captured in a quote that appeared in the *Inlander* in 2013, when the mine was temporarily closed after the community lost two young men in separate mining accidents.

"Mining can be dangerous work, but the people in the Silver Valley live for it. As long as there is silver in the ground, they will dig deeper. No matter now many hits they take, they will always get up and keep working."

THE BITTERROOT LOOP
Nor-Pac Trail

Mullan, Idaho

To ride the next leg of the Bitterroot Loop, find the Northern Pacific Trail (Nor-Pac) sign on the east end of the Trail of the Coeur d'Alenes Mullan Trailhead. Keep an eye out for these markers, because they guide you through the woods to Lookout Pass and beyond to the I-90 Taft Exit #5 in Montana.

Begin the trip by crossing 3rd St. and ride east on Fisher, behind the big brick Athletic Pavilion on the left, until you meet Earle Street. Straight ahead on the right is **Mullan Trail**, a brand new trailside amenity with **cabins** for rent, **RV sites**, and a **convenience store**. The store opens at 4 a.m. This is the place to stop and stock up on food and water, and any other items you will want on the remote sections of trail coming up in the national forests.

Mullan, Idaho

After .2 mile on Earle St., slip onto BL-90. You will temporarily leave the Nor-Pac because it crosses private land. Ride east on BL-90 (Friday Avenue), past the ball park, the interchange, and Lucky Friday mine. See a sign to Larson Rd. 1.5 miles from the trailhead. Get on Larson Road toward Shoshone Park and Hale Fish Hatchery. There is an old dairy at Larson, then another fork at 3.1 miles. Go left .2 mile towards Shoshone Park, where there are **public restrooms**, picnic tables, barbecue grills, and **drinking water**. This day use area is open 6 a.m. to 10 p.m. Hale Fish Hatchery is .3 mile past Shoshone Park. Buy a handful of fish food from the dispenser and **feed the fish**. Go left at the end of the pavement through a little cedar grove. At 3.9 miles, look for the Nor-Pac marker and bear right onto NF-3026 to get back on the multiuse Nor-Pac trail. At mile 5 go under I-90, then ride uphill to Stevens Lake Wayside stop.

Stevens Lake Wayside   Trail Miles: 78.5

WHERE AM I?
You are on NF Rd. 3026 near the trailhead to Stevens Peak in western Shoshone County.

REST STOP AMENITIES: Restroom, Picnic Table, Interpretive Sign, Hiking Trails.
Next Stop: .6 miles

Point of Interest: Stevens Peak (6,838) is the highest mountain in the western reaches of the Bitterroot range. It is a popular destination for climbing, hiking, and back country skiing. Inland Northwest groups often use it for mountaineering training.

After the wayside stop, turn left uphill at the switchback and look for the Nor-Pac sign on the left. Note, the Idaho Centenial Trail and Stevens Lake trail intersect at the hairpin. Willow Creek Rd. also connects here and loops back to Mullan.

Dorsey Trailhead   Trail Miles: 79.1

DRIVING DIRECTIONS: There is no parking at this trailhead.

TRAILHEAD AMENITIES:
Interpretive Sign,
Next Stop: 3.2 miles

Point of Interest: Remnants of an old watering station can be seen on the right. This is where trains refilled water tanks so they didn't run out of steam when chugging over the pass.

Northern Pacific train dangles from the tracks after the "S" bridge collapsed from a snowslide in February 1903, between Saltese, Montana, and Wallace, Idaho. Photo courtesy of Historic WallacePreservation Society.

ELEVATION: 4,738 FT. **Trail Miles:** 82.3 **Lookout Pass Trailhead**

DRIVING DIRECTIONS: Take I-90 to Exit #0. Lookout Pass parking lot is on the south side of the freeway.

TRAILHEAD AMENITIES: Interpretive Sign. (Parking, Restroom, Water, Trail Info, Hiking, Food, Camping, Rentals, Hiawatha Tickets nearby at the lodge).
Next Stop: 11.1 miles

Looking west from Lookout Pass

Lookout Pass Ski & Recreation Area serves as headquarters and visitor center for the Route of the Hiawatha. The lodge is open when the Hiawatha is, from the last weekend of May to the first weekend in October, weather permitting. The lodge has a **bike rental and repair shop,** (bike rack comes w/rental) **restrooms, gift shop, deli & grill** with **hamburgers, sandwiches** and **wraps, beer.** Mountain bikes or hybrids are recommended on the Hiawatha. Make sure everyone in your party has an emergency repair kit with extra tubes. Children under 14 must be with an adult. Helmets and lights are required on the Route of the Hiawatha. Stock up on plenty of **water** and food here as well.

There are several ways to **buy tickets** for the Hiawatha: at the lodge, online at skilookout.com/hiawatha, and from marshals on the trail (who

Copper Lake Trail, Lolo National Forest, in Montana

only accept cash). Tickets are also sold at Scheffy's store in Avery and at the Wallace Inn: $10 adult/$6 child. Six and under are free. If you plan to take the **bus** back up the RoH, pay the $9/$6 when purchasing tickets. There is **free camping** overnight in the Lookout Pass Ski Hill parking lot for self-contained RVs. Call 208.744.1301 or check ridethehiawatha.com.

To reach the Hiawatha, pick up the Nor-Pac trail on the east end of the parking area. You have crossed into Montana's Mineral County and the **Lolo National Forest**. (You have also crossed into the Mountain Time Zone). You will now be riding in the Superior Ranger District of the Lolo National Forest. Check for updates on rules and conditions at fs.usda.gov/alerts/lolo/alerts-notices.

The St. Regis basin opens up before you after .5 mile. Stay left at the fork. There will be a hairpin turn after another .5 mile, and a **hiking/mountain bike trail** to lower St. Regis Lake and some primitive campsites. Another hiking/biking trail leads into the Copper Lake area a mile later. Within two miles, there is a dark and bumpy tunnel. Then you will go under I-90 twice. A half-mile later the trail meets a paved road (Bullion Cr. Rd/NF-507). This is Taft Exit #5 at I-90. Elevation, 3,630 ft.

Go straight until you see the **Route of the Hiawatha sign** to East Portal, Roland, and Pearson Trailheads. You are about 20.5 miles past the Mullan Trailhead. Take Rainey Creek Rd/ NF-506 up to the East Portal turnoff. It's about a 2% grade for 2 miles to the East Portal Trailhead.

If you're ready for a break, the nearest lodgings and supplies are 4.2 miles east at **Mangold's General Store and Motel** in Saltese, Montana. You can continue on the multi-use Nor-Pac Rd. and turn left under the I-90 underpass after 4 miles; or, pedal up to the East Portal Trailhead and catch the new **Route of the Olympian** to Saltese from the

Mangold's in Saltese, MT

northeast corner of the parking lot. The Olympian is non-motorized between here and Saltese from Memorial Day through Labor Day.

Point of Interest: Taft, "The wickedest city in America," blossomed here in 1907, when workers for the Chicago Milwaukee and St. Paul Railroad were blasting and digging the 1.7 mile long tunnel through St. Paul Pass. With 27 saloons and 750 men who toiled in extreme conditions, the town was a magnet for drinkers, gamblers, and prostitutes who were referred to as "canaries." Taft died out when the tunnel was finished, and its remains burned to the ground in the 1910 inferno.

Elevation: 4,147 FT. **Trail Miles: 93.4** **East Portal Trailhead**

DRIVING DIRECTIONS: Take I-90 to the Taft Exit #5 in Montana. Turn left to the Route of the Hiawatha sign. Turn right over the bridge onto NF-506. Drive two miles and turn left on the East Portal cut-off.

TRAILHEAD AMENITIES: Restrooms, Picnic Tables, Interpretive Signs, Route of the Hiawatha and Olympian Trail Access.
Next Stop: 1.9 miles

The 15-mile **Route of the Hiawatha** is in the Rails-to-Trails Conservancy Hall of Fame. It leads gently down a 1.7% grade on the abandoned Milwaukee Road railbed, traversing through ten **tunnels** and seven sky-high **trestles. Interpretive signs** tell about the building of the railroad in this rugged terrain. This non-motorized trail complies with ADA rules for dogs, motorized wheelchairs, and Other Power Driven Mobility Devices (OPDMDs).

The ride begins at the eastern entrance of the cool, drippy, and pitch black 1.7-mile Taft Tunnel, which cuts through the St. Paul Pass from Montana to Idaho. After riding a short way, the tunnel bends and you will be able to see a tiny but comforting point of light on the other end. Stay in your lane to the right, but keep away from the edges to avoid falling into the ditches that drain water from the tunnel. You will enter Idaho and the Pacific Time Zone half way through. The extremely steep 1.9-mile NF-506 Rd. to Roland Summit (elevation: 5,180) leads over the mountain which the Taft Tunnel passes through. At the top, the 506 Road crosses State Line Road into Idaho. It's 3.9 miles downhill from there to the other end of the Taft Tunnel and Roland Trailhead, and the 3-mile multi-use portion of the RoH, where you may occasionally encounter vehicles, particularly the buses that shuttle people and bikes up the mountain from Pearson Trailhead.

Roland Trailhead Trail Miles: 95.3 Elevation: 4150 FT.

DRIVING DIRECTIONS: Take I-90 to the Taft Exit #5 in Montana. Turn left to the Route of the Hiawatha sign. Turn right over the bridge onto NF-506. Drive 7.5 miles over the pass to Roland Trailhead.

TRAILHEAD AMENITIES: Restrooms, Picnic Tables, Interpretive Sign, Parking, Shuttle Bus Stop. **Next Stop: 4.8 miles**

Adair Trailhead Trail Miles: 100.1 Elevation: 3.707 FT.

DRIVING DIRECTIONS: Take I-90 to Wallace Exit #61 and turn left on I-90 Business Loop. Turn right on Fifth St. and right on Cedar St., left on First St., and right on Bank St. This turns into NF-456 (Moon Pass Rd.) The pavement ends after about a mile. At about 18 miles turn left onto Loop Creek Rd/NF-326 to the Adair Trailhead.

ALTERNATE DRIVING DIRECTIONS: Take I-90 to the Rose Lake Exit #34 on the eastern side of 4th of July Pass. Drive 32 miles on SR-3 to NF-50 (St. Joe River Rd.). Continue 47 miles to Avery and turn left onto NF-456 (Moon Pass Rd.). Go past the Pearson Trailhead .4 mile, then turn right onto Loop Creek Rd/NF-326 to Adair Trailhead.

TRAILHEAD AMENITIES: Parking, Restrooms, Interpretive Sign
Next Stop: 8.5 miles

Point of Interest: When gazing out at the vast wilderness, it's hard to believe that lively settlements once dotted the tracks between Taft and Avery. Roland had a two-story train depot, several large bunkhouses, and even a ski hill. Goups came by train from Spokane, Coeur d'Alene, Missoula, and Avery to enjoy a day on the slopes.

The waterfall outside the Taft Tunnel feeds Cliff Creek, which tumbles down to meet Loop Creek. The remote settlements of Grand Forks and Falcon mushroomed where the creeks converge on the valley floor. Falcon had a small store, post office, a forest ranger station, and even a jewelry store.

Grand Forks was a Wild West town mainly comprised of saloons and "sporting" women facilities. It was served by the Spokane Saloon, Old Crow Saloon, North Pole Saloon & Restaurant, Log Cabin Saloon, Anheuser Hotel & Saloon, El Rey Hotel & Saloon, and Bon Ton Restaurant. It also contained the Kelly brothers' Bitterroot Mercantile, a post office, barber shop, and a small emergency hospital. Forest service officials were on a constant campaign to eradicate alcohol sales from the town. But alcoholic beverages were in great demand by railroad construction workers who toiled in extremely demanding conditions, and the prohibition only succeeded in driving sales underground.

The town of Grand Forks, Idaho, has completely disappeared. The Bitter Root Mercantile is front left and the Anheuser Hotel & Saloon is at the end of the street. Photo courtesy of Montana Historical Society Research Center Photograph Archives, Helena, MT

Pearson Trailhead Elevation; 3,175 FT. **Trail Miles: 108.6**

Riders wait to board a bus at Pearson Trailhead, back up to Roland Trailhead

DRIVING DIRECTIONS: I-90 to Wallace Exit #61, turn left on the I-90 Business Loop. Turn right on Fifth St. and right on Cedar St., left on First St., and right on Bank St. This turns into NF-456 (Moon Pass Rd.) The pavement ends after about a mile. At 18.5 miles you will see a Route of the Hiawatha sign. Turn to access Pearson Trailhead, which is .5 mile up the road.

ALTERNATE DRIVING DIRECTIONS: Take I-90 to the Rose Lake Exit #34 on the eastern side of 4th of July Pass. Drive 32 miles on SR-3 to NF-50 (St. Joe River Rd.). Continue 47 miles to Avery and turn left onto NF-456 (Moon Pass Rd.). It's 9 miles to the Pearson Trailhead.

TRAILHEAD AMENITIES: Parking, Restrooms, Picnic Tables, Interpretive Sign, Shuttle Bus back to Roland Trailhead. (Primitive camping nearby). **Next Stop: 10.8 miles**

Many cyclists ride down from the Taft Tunnel then catch the **shuttle bus** back up the mountain at Pearson Trailhead. Start your ride by noon if you want to take your time and not worry about missing the last bus. Bus service times are reduced in September, so check the schedule when making plans. Some who choose to pedal back up instead prefer to park at Pearson and ride the 1.7% uphill first, then reward themselves with a nice relaxing downhill ride. If you think the 15-mile experience is over too quickly and wish the trail was longer, here are some ideas on how to extend the fun.

There is free **dispersed (primitive) camping** near Pearson Trailhead along Loop Creek. To camp there, go down the trailhead access road, turn right (north) on Moon Pass Rd./NF-456, and ride .4 mile to Loop Creek Rd/NF-326. Turn right toward Moss Creek and Roland. Watch for the shuttle buses and other traffic. If you've paid to ride the shuttle bus, you can ask to be dropped off at the camping area. If you plan to have a fire, you will have to pack a collapsible shovel and collapsible five-gallon water container, because shovels and water are required for campfires at undeveloped sites in the forest. For forest alerts and updates in Idaho, see fs.usda.gov/alerts/ipnf/alerts-notices, or call 208.245.4517.

The nearest outpost of **civilization** is Avery, Idaho, nine miles from Pearson Trailhead by way of Moon Pass Rd. Moon Pass Rd. is one of two options for getting to Avery. The second is the Old Milwaukee Scenic/Alternate Route, which is the recommended route laid out by the Friends of the Coeur d'Alene Trails as part of the 300k Bitterroot Loop. It's 1.8-miles longer than the Moon Pass option and the road is a bit rougher, but it's also closer to the river and less traveled by vehicles. Both roads straddle the North Fork of the St. Joe River.

If you go on the Old Milwaukee Route, exit down the Pearson Trailhead access road and turn right (north) onto Moon Pass Rd. Turn west at .4 mile, and take the bridge across the North Fork of the St. Joe River. Then turn left again onto the Milwaukee Route/Rd-1997, a single lane gravel road with pullouts.

Another road called NF-1997 intersects two miles south. It leads to the **Arid Peak Fire Lookout.** You can spend the night in the historical USFS **Arid Peak Lookout**, which

was built at 5,306 feet in 1934 to help detect fires, especially those sparked by the Milwaukee Railroad. Rental of the 20-foot high fire lookout starts at $25/night. Features include two cots with mattresses, dishes, propane lantern, propane camp stove, water containers, replica fire finder, wood stove, and 360 degree views. You supply the bedding and propane. Water must be hauled in or fetched from a stream and treated. There is an outhouse nearby. Find Arid Peak up the second NF-1997 Rd. Turn right (west) and travel about 6.5 miles to Trailhead #175. If driving, park at the wide spot there. Then

Waterfall along Moon Pass Rd. to Avery there is a moderate 3-mile hike on

Avery, Idaho

Forest service trails. Demand is high for fire lookout lodgings. Call the ranger station at 208.245.4517 for reservations.

Continuing on the Milwaukee Route, you will see a tressle over the river at 5.6 miles. Go under it and ride another .5 mile farther to **Telichpah Campground**. The campground is on the North Fork of the St. Joe River. It has five small camping units with fireplaces or grills and picnic tables, but no drinking water. **Restrooms** are vault toilets and trash must be packed out. RV trailers are not recommended.

This is a trailhead for the Nelson Peak National Recreation Trail System. **Hike** and **mountain bike** on Telichpah Creek Trail #196, which connects to Nelson Ridge Trail #186. Camping is free on a first-come-first-served basis. Call the St. Joe Ranger District, 208.245.2531. The country here is beautiful and rugged, so come prepared with everything you need to survive. Bears like it too, so keep a clean and odor-free camp. Get all kinds of bear information at bebearaware.org.

You can also get to Avery and Telichpah Campground via Moon Pass Rd., where you will see **waterfalls** and ride through more old train **tunnels.** Head down the access road from Pearson Trailhead and turn left on Moon Pass Rd. This unpaved road is the main route between Avery and Wallace, so expect some vehicles, along with dust clouds if the weather is dry. After five miles you will cross a bridge over the North Fork of the St. Joe River. Keep going straight on Moon Pass Rd. to get to Avery. If you're camping at **Telichpah Campground** turn right after crossing the bridge, ride downhill and turn right again on the Old Milwaukee Rd. It's .5 mile to the camp.

Tunnel on the Moon Pass Rd.

The Milwaukee route continues from the south end of the campground and the road gets rougher on this stretch. It's 4.5 more miles to the main stem of the St. Joe River and the St. Joe River Rd./NF-50. Turn right and ride another .1 mile into Avery.

With more than 100 miles of free-flowing river, "The Joe" offers a variety of experiences from a gentle float, to hardcore **Class IV and V rapids.** See what rafting on The Joe looks like at rowadventures.com. The Joe is also known as a world-class fly fishery. As you ride along it you will likely see fisherman in the water gracefully casting their lines.

THE BITTERROOT LOOP
Old Milwaukee Road

ELEVATION: 2,440 FT.   **Trail Miles: 119.4   Avery, Idaho**

DRIVING DIRECTIONS: If coming from east of 4th of July Pass: take I-90 to the Rose Lake Exit #34. Drive south 32 miles on Hwy 3 to NF-50 (St. Joe River Rd.). Turn left and continue 47 miles to Avery.

ALTERNATE DRIVING DIRECTIONS: From Spokane: take I-90 Sandpoint/Moscow exit to Hwy 95 south and drive 31 miles to Plummer. Turn left on SR-5 and go 18 miles to St. Maries. Follow the road to the east end of downtown. Immediately after the curve with the Logger Memorial, turn left and go one block to the four-way stop, then left again over the St. Joe River bridge. Drive .6 mile, and turn right onto St. Joe River Rd.NF-50. Follow the river 47 miles to Avery.

AMENITIES: Restroom (open during business hrs.), Lodging, Shopping, Museum, Post Office, Roadside Attractions. (Camping, Showers, Laundry, Water, Food, Phones nearby). **Next Stop: 12.8 miles.**

Avery, Idaho, (pop. 50, more or less) is nestled in the St. Joe River valley, surrounded by thousands of acres of forested wilderness. Once a busy railroad stop and logging town, Avery is a year-round base camp for kayakers, fishermen, hunters, hikers, and snowmobilers. It's the place to rest up before continuing toward St. Maries. Find lodgings, a hot shower, supplies, and a bite to eat. There is no cell service here, just old-fashioned land lines.

Point of Interest: Only a handful of settlers lived here until 1907, when construction began on the Pacific extension of the Milwaukee railroad.

See **Scheffy's Motel** and **convenience store** when heading west along the St. Joe River Rd. The motel rooms sleep up to six and include full kitchens. The public may use the **bathhouse** for $6. It has both **tubs and showers**. Add $2 if you need a towel. There is also a coin-op **laundry**. People riding the RoH from Pearson can get **tickets** to the Route of the Hiawatha in the store. 208.245.4410

The **Idaho Fly Fishing Company** is across the road. Get outfitted for fly fishing and meet the owner, Dan, an avid road cyclist who has pedaled across the U.S. and enjoys sharing his story with fellow riders. Find coffee service inside with deli-style sandwiches, hard ice cream, and shakes, with huckleberry being the most popular. Open daily 8 a.m. to 6 p.m. Memorial Day to Labor Day. 208.245.3626.

Avery, Idaho

You will find a **gift shop** and several **roadside attractions** in the heart of Avery, such as the old **Milwaukee Road dining car, historical museum, jail** and **trout pond**. The **public restroom** and museum are open during post office hours. The trout pond is a favorite stop. Buy a handful of fish food for 25 cents and watch them eat.

Avery Gift Shop is across the street from Avery's roadside attractions. Stop in for **huckleberry** treats, local crafts, and **souvenirs** with hunting, railroad, and Avery themes. Relax outside at the picnic table or around the fire pit. A modern and reasonably priced **vacation suite** above the gift shop sleeps eight. There is a bed-

There is a modern vacation rental above the gift shop in this Old West style building across from Avery's roadside attractions

room with two queen beds, another with two twins, and room for two more on the sofa sleeper in the living room. The lodgings include **satellite TV**, **air conditioning**, and **free local phone service**. Make sure to have a calling card in your survival kit. The kitchen is stocked with dishes, utensils, pots and pan; everything but the food. See averygiftshop.com for reservations, or 208.245.1308, and 208.245.2055 after hours.

If you are staying at **Cabins By The Joe & RV Park,** head west from the Avery Gift Shop on Siberts Old River Rd. It's a .5 mile ride over the bridge, past the old Avery school and along the river to the cabins. See cabinsbythejoe.com, or call 425. 773.3724 for reservations.

The old Avery school, built in 1923, has been purchased and is being converted to the **Avery Schoolhouse B&B**, opening sometime before July 4th. It will have five bedrooms with private baths and offer a country farm breakfast, light lunch, and casual, beanery-style dinner for $150/night double occupancy. There is no restaurant in Avery but these folks won't let you go hungry. Call for info: 208.245.2450.

At this point of the journey, you will have to decide whether to continue on the unpaved multi-use route laid out by the Friends of the Coeur d'Alene Trails, or would you prefer to cruise the 47 miles to St. Maries on the paved St. Joe River Rd/NF-50? The paved road is faster,

Avery, Idaho

less dusty, and has more amenities, but you will be competing for road space with log trucks and recreational vehicles pulling trailers. The lack of decent shoulders results in less than ideal riding conditions, mainly because the average rural north Idaho driver, who has no problem attempting to dodge deer, moose, dogs, and various birds in the road on a regular basis, finds it unusual to slow down for, or go around, cyclists.

That said, the chart at right shows distances to amenities on the St. Joe River Rd. between Avery and St. Maries. Those following the route prescribed by the Friends group will still be able to reach these services from an occasional bridge or access road and biking a few extra miles.

ST. JOE RIVER RD.
Avery to St. Maries

Avery	0
Vault Toilet Restroom	1.2
USFS Ranger Station	6.0
Marble Creek Day Use	12.2
St. Joe Lodge	12.8
Spring Creek Cabins	14.3
BLM Huckleberry Campground	16.5
Calder Store Turn Off	22.4
Big Eddy Hotel/ Campground & Rest-Bar	27.6
Shadowy St. Joe Campground	37
St. Maries	47

Siberts Old River Rd, turns to packed gravel just beyond Cabins by the Joe. There is a pedestrian bridge 5.9 miles later, which leads to the Avery Ranger Station (208.245.4517). Find **visitor information** and a **public restroom** there. Back on the trail, stay along the river. You will come out at the St. Joe River Rd. 12.8 miles past Avery. Turn left for the Marble Creek Interpretive Center (.2 mile west).

Trail Miles: 132.2 Marble Creek Interpretive Center
ELEVATION: 2,280 FT.

DRIVING DIRECTIONS: See directions for Avery, Idaho. Marble Creek is 34 miles up NF-50 (The St. Joe River Rd.).

AMENITIES: Restroom/Accessible, Water, Picnic Tables, Interpretive Displays, Parking, Swimming **Next Stop: 9.5 miles**

See **historical photos** and **artifacts**, and read about early 20th century logging methods. The interpretive center is a gateway to historic Marble Creek. A dirt road leads south to 60 miles of backcountry mountain trails and relics of the area's log-

THE BITTERROOT LOOP
Old Milwaukee Road

ging legacy, including homestead cabins, steam donkey engines, and the **Hobo Cedar Grove** hiking trail. This rest stop is for day use only, and it is a popular spot for river floaters to put their tubes and rafts in.

Wooden Plank Bridge over The St. Joe River near Marble Creek.

Turn west out of the parking lot onto St. Joe River Rd/NF-50, and take a right after .25 mile, over the wood plank bridge to the north side of the river. Make a left onto Potlatch Rd., the Old Milwaukee right of way, and follow the sign toward Big Creek and Calder.

Watch for moose, eagle, and other wildlife in the wetlands along the river. At 4.6 miles you come to the 515-foot Herrick Tunnel (No. 37). There is a nice turnout at the entrance to pull over and enjoy the view. Look for Big Creek Bridge 1.2 miles past the tunnel. The town of Herrick was to the right. Ride another 4 miles to Calder.

If you want **food** and **lodgings** at **St. Joe Lodge**, call first, then ride .6 miles past Marble Creek on the St. Joe River Rd./NF-50. They will serve lunch and dinner to those who make advance arrangements. There are two **bedrooms** for $60/night: one sleeps two, the other four. The shared bath has a clawfoot tub. They will cook breakfast on request for lodging guests for an additional charge. Play a game of shuffle board and hang out around the riverside fire pit. Get a sandwich and water for the remote section of trail ahead. Make reservations at 208.245.2284.

The Herrick Tunnel on the Old Milwaukee Rd.

Spring Creek Cabins are 2 miles past Marble Creek on the St. Joe River Rd. They can accommodate twenty people. Bathing facilities are in the community shower house. There is a **public telephone** here for use with your calling card.

Huckleberry Camground is 4.3 miles past Marble Creek at MP 32. Go 6 more miles to the Calder turn-off. Managed by the BLM.

ELEVATION: 2,240 FT. **Trail Miles: 141.7** **Calder, Idaho**

DRIVING DIRECTIONS: See directions for Avery, Idaho. The Calder turnoff is 23.3 miles up The St. Joe River Rd./NF-50.

AMENITIES: Restroom, Water, Picnic Area, Parking, Camping, Food, Post Office.
Next Stop: 24 miles

The main thing in Calder is the **Calder Store, a combination restaurant, lounge,** and small **convenience store** open daily in summer. Get scoop ice cream, drinks, AA batteries, chocolate bars, firewood, and camping food like hot dogs and marshmallows. Arrive at the restaurant before noon to order a hearty breakfast such as **huckleberry pancakes** and eggs. They serve good home-cooked dinners. There is **free tent camping** in the grassy area out back.

Three-fourths of a mile down the trail from Calder is a weak link on this loop in the form of a bridge with cement baricades due to fire damage. Some people walk their bikes across the charred timbers. (You may encounter large puddles for a few miles past the bridge). An alternative is to get on the paved St. Joe River Rd/NF-50 at Calder and ride 7.7 miles to reconnect with the Potlatch Rd./Milwaukee route. Either that, or follow this circuitous up and down detour, also explained on the Friends of the Coeur

The author checks the burned out bridge near Calder

d'Alenes Trails Web site. From Calder Store, turn right, then immediately left onto First St. Cross a cattle guard. It's flat for about a mile, then there is a hairpin left turn uphill. After 4 miles there is a sharp left turnoff that leads back down to Potlatch Rd.

After 3.6 miles you will pass under the St. Joe River Rd. and come to a fork. Stay left and ride over the trestle bridge. After another 3 miles you will come to the junction of St. Joe City Rd. and Potlatch Rd. Today, this is just a quiet backwoods intersection, but back in the day, two rollicking frontier towns flourished here.

Point of Interest: St Joe City marks the head of navigation on the St. Joe River, the highest navigable river in the world. Before St. Joe City was established, the city of Ferrell boomed to 1,000 people on the north side of the river in the late 1880s. Logging activity was in full swing and the river was a frenzied lane of travel with logs floating down and steamboats full of fortune hunters, gamblers, lumber barons, sightseers,

THE BITTERROOT LOOP
Old Milwaukee Road

Bill Ferrell and family with two Native American women at Ferrell, c. 1910.
Photo courtesy Museum of North Idaho.

and settlers riding up. Ferrell had hotels, stores, a theater, bank, floating hospital, and saloons with "houses" upstairs, where over 30 prostitutes parted men from their hard-earned pay. But when the railroad laid its tracks on the south side of the river, a new town called St. Joe City sprang up around the depot and Ferrell disappeared The film, *The Tornado,* was filmed in St. Joe City in 1925. There are no vistor amenities in St. Joe City today.

If you can't make it to St. Maries and are prepared for **camping,** turn right on St. Joe City Rd., go .7 mile, then left on the St. Joe River Rd./NF-50 and 2.2 miles to the USFS Shadowy St. Joe Campground. It has vault **toilets, drinking water, firewood** for sale, and a host. There are no showers but you can take a dip in the river. 208.245.4517.

Back on the trail, Potlatch Rd. turns into Railroad Grade Rd. east of the St. Joe City Rd. junction. After 11 miles, you'll cross railroad tracks and come out on the paved Milwaukee Rd. Turn right (west) .8 mile to State Route 3 (SR-3), the *White Pine Scenic Byway.* After 165 miles on the Bitterroot Loop, you will now switch from dedicated and multiuse trails to state highway riding. Downtown St. Maries and lodging options are to the right, across the bridge over the St. Maries River.

ELEVATION: 2,127 FT. **Trail Miles: 165.7** **St. Maries, Idaho**

DRIVING DIRECTIONS: If coming from east of 4th of July Pass: take I-90 to the Rose Lake Exit #34. Drive south 32.7 miles on SR-3 to St. Maries.

From Spokane: On I-90 take Sandpoint/ Moscow exit to Hwy 95 south and drive 31 miles to Plummer. Turn left on SR-5 and drive 18 miles to St. Maries.

AMENITIES: (Restroom, Water, Picnic Area, Interpretive Signs, Food, Lodging, Camping, Swimming, Shopping, Museum, Mural Tour, Rentals, Laundry, Post Office nearby). **Next Stop: 12 miles**.

Logger Memorial, St. Maries, Idaho

St. Maries, (pronounced *Mary's*) pop. 2,333, at the confluence of the St. Joe and St. Maries Rivers, is the Benewah County seat, and the largest city in the county.

The remainder of the Loop goes through downtown St. Maries, then west to Heyburn Park on SR-5, a winding two-lane commuter route with narrow shoulders. **Fort Hemenway Manor** and the **Pines Motel** both offer a **courtesy shuttle** back to Heyburn Park for their guests. Since these are courtesy shuttles, they are more or less at the owner's convenience. There are also **paid shuttle** options. See *Service Providers* on page 114. Arrangements for all shuttles need to be made in advance. This guide will describe what to expect if you are cycling to Heyburn, but first, let's take a tour of St. Maries.

Point of Interest: An entry in the Federal Writers' Project of 1950 describes St. Maries as "sprawled on hills and almost lost to itself." The remote quality noted by the writer persists. It makes the visitor to St. Maries feel as though they have stepped back a few decades in time. The city has no big box stores and there isn't even a stoplight. The people here are friendly and they love their family-centered rural lifestyle.

For **Harvest Foods** grocery store and **Riverbend Laundry**, turn left onto State Route 3 (SR-3) from Milwaukee Rd. The owner of Harvest Foods, Chester, says it's okay for cycle travelers to come in and use the **restroom**, which is right inside the main entrance. He also lets people **park their RVs** in the lot when they are riding the trails, but they need to contact him to make arrangements in advance by calling 208.245. 6555. Harvest Foods is a full-service **grocery store** with a sec-

St. Maries, Idaho

tion of handy cycle-sized **camping items** on a display near the deli. They carry things like mosquito sticks, tent pole repair kits, and fire starter—items you may need when camping in north Idaho. Check out the historic photos on the walls. The "River through the Lakes" mural on the side of the building is one of seventeen around town that depict scenes from St. Maries' past. The Riverbend **Laundry** on the other end of the Harvest Foods parking lot is open 24 hours.

Casa de Oro Restaurant, St. Maries Golf Course

There is a **Casa de Oro** Mexican Restaurant tucked against a hillside on the southern edge of town. Dine inside or on the deck overlooking the St. Maries Golf Course and a **scenic** back-drop of beautiful mountains. Take SR-3 south .4 mile and turn left up Golf Course Rd. It's uphill for about a mile to the nicest restaurant in town, and worth the effort.

Owner, Marco, says the *Arroz con Pollo, Pollo con Crema,* and *Carne Asada,* are among the most popular dishes. They are traditional family recipes brought from Jalisco, Mexico. The menu includes hamburgers for those desiring American fare. There is a full-service lounge here. Summer hours are 11 a.m. to 10 p.m, with a daily lunch special for $5.95 year-round. Call 208.245.3200.

To reach downtown St. Maries, ride west on the bridge over the St. Maries River toward **Archie's IGA**, which has a **Subway** inside. You will also see **Zips** here. That is the extent of fast food in St. Maries. Apparently there is an ordinance against it and these two are exceptions.

The street becomes College Ave. Turn right onto First for the **River Front Suites** on the St. Joe River. Each of the fully furnished and non-smoking suites can accommodate four to six people. They are spacious, clean, and cozy with **rustic log furniture**, futons, 32" flat screen TVs with DirectTV and DVD Player, free Wifi, and complete **kitchens**. They recently added suites that are a little cheaper, but they don't have the awesome river view, so if you want to gaze at the water, make sure to mention it when making your reservation. Also, if you are traveling with a dog, let them know when reserving so they can put you in the doggie room.

St. Maries, Idaho

Bud's Burgers, a half block west, is a favorite among the locals for breakfast, plus, you can still get a burger there for $5. They also offer homemade pies and serve a bean veggie burger made from scratch. The **Junction Drive-In**, one block east, has burgers, sandwiches, Mexican-style food, and ice cream treats. Check out the vintge OrderMatic."

If you go north over the bridge at the Junction Drive-In, then take the first left, you will see a sign for **swimming** and **picnicking**. This is the way to access **Aqua Park** without riding through town.

There is a pleasant 15-mile out and back ride along the St. Maries River, heading south on First. The pavement ends two miles out. It is mostly flat with a few short hills the last three miles. At 7.7 miles, go left at the fork to enjoy beautiful spots along the river and former St. Maries railroad tracks. There are a few residences along the way but no services, so take food and water with you.

Point of Interest: St. Maries was occupied by federal troops when martial law was declared to quell union protests over harsh conditions in the lumber camps. You can read about it on the interpretive sign at the corner of College and First.

St. Maries, Idaho

To stay at **Fort Hemenway Manor**, continue west on College. You will come upon Benewah County Courthouse on the right, a building on the National Register of Historic Places, with the Ten Commandments still on the lawn. There are **pubic restrooms** downstairs. The auto licensing office in the right corner of the lobby has St. Maries' best display of **historical photos** from the steamboat and logging days. The friendly clerks don't mind when visitors stop in just to view the pictures. The **post office** is one block south of the courthouse on Seventh St. For the **St. Maries Library** with free **Wifi,** continue west on College another block. To reach the manor, turn left on Ninth St., ride south one block to Jefferson, then turn right one block to Tenth St.

Fort Hemenway Manor commands a stately presence on the corner of Tenth and Jefferson. The home was completed in 1913 for lumber baron Fred Hemenway and features beveled glass windows, custom English chandeliers, oak floors with intricate walnut inlay, beamed ceilings, a fireplace trimmed with Italian tile, and antique furnishings throughout. A tasteful blend of present and past, you may enjoy a movie in the entertainment room, or gather in the formal living room where a guest might perform an impromptu number on the upright grand piano. Rest in one of four carefully appointed rooms, where bed sheets are pressed in an antique mangle. Absorb tranquil views of the surrounding mountains from any of the bedrooms or from a shady spot on the porch.

In the morning your hostess, Gigi, will prepare a full-course **gourmet breakfast** with selections such as: huckleberry scones, fire roasted veggie frittata, tabouli scrambled eggs, or apple stuffed French toast. There is **free Internet** in the manor, and **secure bicycle storage**

Fort Hemenway Manor

1001 W. Jefferson Avenue ~208-245-7979
forthemenwaymanor.com

is inside on the lower level. There is also a furnished studio option downstairs for short or long-term stays. If a **courtesy shuttle** between the Trail of the Coeur d'Alenes and St. Maries is desired, please inquire when making reservations.

Look down the hill on Tenth to see the main entrance to **Aqua Park** in the distance. You can **swim** there in the St. Joe River and have lunch at a **picnic** table.

St. Maries, Idaho

The **restroom** at the gate is open seasonally.

The Brickwall Spa on the corner of Tenth and Main is an eclectic beauty salon that sells espresso, wines, some clothes, and sometimes hosts live music events.

My Kitchen is in the former Handi Corner space. It's a straighforward small town **restaurant** with friendly service and a decent selection of basic American food, such as steaks, cod, oysters, liver and onions, homemade soup, and pie for dessert. They open at 6 a.m. seven days a week.

The gate in the dike at St. Maries Aqua Park can be closed in the event of flooding

One of St. Maries' newest and favorite gathering spots is the **Grapple Haus** tap house on Tenth St. and Center. They have 21 brews on tap, plus cider and a wide selection of wines. Sit under an umbrella on the inviting deck and enjoy the view of the forested hillside across the river. The tap house has menus from restaurants around town. Order from: Main Street Bistro, Gem State Grill, Pizza Factory, Bud's Burgers, Heidi's, or Casa de Oro, and your meal will be delivered. Follow them at grapplehauson10th on Facebook.for entertainment updates.

There is a new espresso cafe called **Always Grounded** a block from Aqua Park with a good variety of coffee drinks, teas, cider, smoothies

St. Maries, Idaho

and specialty drinks, along with scones, bagels,and muffins. They open at 6 a.m. on weekdays and 7 on weekends.

Point of Interest: In the early days, when the main form of transortation in this area was by water, St. Maries' main business district sprang up on the shore of the St. Joe River. Steamboats from Coeur d'Alene pulled in three times a day, dropping off people and frieght, and boarding more for the return trip up the lake.

On the way to Aqua Park on Tenth St. you will pass the **historic railroad depot**, built in 1908. The main line of the Chicago, Milwaukee, and Puget Sound Railroad came through until 1980.The **interpretive sign** at the railroad depot suggests the the townfolk felt their city merited a more opulent depot and notes their displeasure with the building's modest design.

During St. Maries' heyday, thousands of rugged lumberjacks rode the trains bound for the woods to work in what has been called "the most dangerous occupation in America." On a typical day you would have seen a hundred such men on the streets of St. Maries, uniformly dressed in woolen shirts and hats, mackinaws, and wool pants "sawed off" at the tops of caulked boots.

St. Maries waterfront c.1910. Steamer Seattle at the dock and houseboats tied along the shore. Photo courtesy Museum of North Idaho.

St. Maries, Idaho

Back on Main Street between Eighth and Ninth, **The Paperhouse,** carries a good selection of books on **local history**. Stop in there to see the **Gallery on Main**, which features a small display of works by area jewelers, scultptors, and painters.

Main Street Bistro & Espresso two doors east, offers **pizzas** (from personal to supreme) with vegetarian, **gluten free**, and thin crust options; and pasta boats with choices of seafood and chicken alfredo, chicken pesto, sausage pepper bake, lasagna, and crab ravioli. There are five varieties of wraps, salads, soups, bread sticks, a small selection of sandwiches, along with **beer and wine** offerings. They have a full selection of **espresso** flavors, **homemade fudge, Dreyers ice cream,** and free **Wifi**. This downtown business is open daily year round from 7 a.m. to at least 8 p.m., and sometimes longer.

Start early if you want to browse the stores on Main Ave., because most close shortly after 5 p.m. Likewise, most places are closed Sundays.

Cycle down the hill on Main to the **Hughes House Museum** where St. Maries' history is preserved in the 1902 log cabin that originally served as a men's club, then as the home and office of Doc. Thompson. The Milwaukee, St. Paul, Puget Sound railroad car displayed in the yard commemorates the line that came through between 1909 and 1980. An Idaho Ponderosa Pine in the yard was grown from a seed that took a trip to outer space and back. The museum opens in summer Wed. through Sun., 12 to 4 p.m., "if the volunteers can make it," as the brochure says.

Pizzas
Wraps
Pasta Boats
Sandwiches
Salads
Soups
Beer & Wine
Ice Cream
Espresso
Fudge

OPEN
DAILY
7 am-8 pm

806 Main Ave, St. Maries, ID
208-245-5539

BITTERROOT LOOP
State Route Five

St. Maries, Idaho

The **Logger Memorial**, a block east of the museum on Main Ave. honors those who lost their lives in the most dangerous profession. Lumber built St. Maries and it is still a major force of the economy here. The city is fiercely proud of its logging heritage, evident by the logging- themed roadside attractions and historical photos displayed around town, in stores, at the courthouse, pictured on some of the 17 murals, and commemorated during the annual Paul Bunyan days celebration on Labor Day weekend. More lumbering history is enshrined at **Mullan Trail Park,** which you will encounter by going west on Main Ave., past the Paul Bunyan statue that has towered over the grade school and neighborhood since 1967.

The **Pines Motel** is on Main and Twelfth St. right across from the **city park** and **pool.** The motel has clean, quiet, air conditioned rooms, each with a mini-fridge, microwave, flat screen cable TV, phone, free Wifi, and firm beds. **Free coffee** and hot chocolate are available anytime. The entire motel is **smoke-free.** Ask about a **courtesy shuttle** between St. Maries and the Trail of the Coeur d'Alenes in Heyburn State Park when making reservations.

Continue west on Main, past Paul Bunyan, and ride uphill for several blocks to Mullan Trail Park. The "steam donkey" here is an example of the wood or oil fueled steam powered generators that were hauled into the woods to skid logs. This steam donkey once operated in the Hobo Creek area, up Marble Creek.

Mullan Park has a large kiosk in a gazebo with an **interpretive display** where you can learn about timber stands in the St. Joe Valley and early years of logging. The **restroom** is open seasonally. Water spigots in the park are locked up.

The statue of John Mullan is one of six in Idaho that commemorate the building of the Mullan Military Road

Cabin City, across from Mullan Park, is now Cabin City Q, a **barbecue restaurant** that smokes ribs, chicken, pulled pork, brisket, and prime rib on site. They're open from 11 am to 7 pm. 208.245.0785.

Proceed west on SR-5 and enjoy the beautiful scenery as you take advantage of some downhill coasting over the next stretch to Heyburn Park. There is a broad turnount after six miles, which overlooks the St. Joe River valley. Benewah Rd. leads south. Cell service is spotty on the stretch coming up, so make calls before heading down the hill.

At the bottom of the hill, before crossing the bridge over Benewah Creek, make a right onto Benewah Lake Rd. to access one of three campgrounds in Heyburn State Park. Benewah Campground has tent and RV camping with showers on a first come first served basis. Sites cost about $30/night. The campground is sightly over a mile from SR-5. Call park headqurters for information at 208.686.1308.

Chatcolet Bridge comes into view a few miles after the Benewah hill.

One tenth of a mile past Benewah Creek Rd. is **Alvin's RV Park** on the left, where you can reserve the **camping cabin** or pitch a tent. The cabin has a table and chairs, and bunkbeds. You will need to provide your own bedding. Guests can **shower** free, do **laundry**, and use the free **wifi**. Bring food because there are no services. 208.245.5879.

Point of Interest: The grass growing in the lake with watery paths cut through it is wild rice that was planted several decades ago by waterfowl hunters to improve habitat. St. Maries Wild Rice Co. (now based in Oregon) harvests the certified organic rice in September and sells it online and through various distributors.

As the road hugs the lakeshore, Chatcolet Bridge will soon come into view. 2.3 miles after Benewah Lake Rd. you will come to a sign that explains how the St. Joe River flows between two lakes, and that it's the highest

Wild rice in the lake

navigable river in the world. The elevation here is 2,307 ft. After another 1.8 miles, look for the **Rocky Point** day use area.

Trail Miles: 177.7 **Rocky Point Day Use Area**
ELEVATION: 2,128 FT.

DRIVING DIRECTIONS: From I-90 take HWY 95 south 32 miles to SR-5. Head east seven miles to the park entrance. You may want to turn left on Chatcolet Rd. at six miles to get a parking permit.

AMENITIES: Restroom/Accessible, Water, Picnic Area, Interpretive Signs, Parking/ADA/RV, Swimming, Rentals, Seasonal C-Store. **Next Stop: 1 mile**

Rocky Point is part of Heyburn State Park and a nice place to take a break, go for a swim, and read the interpretive signs about the CCC camp projects. There is a tiny store where you can rent a kayak, canoe, or padde boat.

Ride a mile past Rocky Point, and turn right to Chatcolet Rd. for Heyburn State Park Headquarters. It's another 1.2 miles to complete the loop at Indian Cliffs. If you came down from Plummer you've got a 6-mile uphill ride still ahead. A big congratulations to those who rode the 300k Bitterroot Loop! Come back soon with your friends and family!

THE BITTERROOT LOOP
Service Providers

Information About Area Cycle Trails

Trail of the Coeur d'Alenes/The Coeur d'Alenes Old Mission State Park, Kathleen Durfee, Manager–208.682.3814. OLD@idpr.idaho.gov parksandrecreation.idaho.gov
Trail of the Coeur d'Alenes/Coeur d'Alene Tribe, Jason Brown, Manager–208.686.1118
Trail of the Coeur d'Alenes/Heyburn State Park, Ron Hise, Ranger–208.686.1308
South Lake Promotions, Inc.; southlakecda.com/trail.htm
Friends of the Coeur d'Alene Trails; friendsofcoeurdalenetrails.org
Spokane Centennial Trail–509.624.7188; spokanecentennialtrail.org
North Idaho Centennial Trail–208.292.1634; www.northidahocentennialtrail.org
Route of the Hiawatha–208.744.1301; www.skilookout.com

Get to the Trails Without Driving

LOCAL TRAIL TOURING SERVICE

ROW Adventures–866.836.9340; rowadventurecenter.com. During the summer ROW Adventures offers guided group tours on the Trail of the Coeur d'Alenes and Hiawatha Trail. On these day trips guests learn about the Coeur d'Alene Indians, Jesuit missionaries, fur trappers, mining history, early pioneers, and more. Transport to/from Coeur d'Alene is included. If you would like a longer excursion check out ROWs 5-day Bitterroot Bonanza. Starting in Spokane this trip combines bike touring on three dedicated cycling trails, rafting on the Clark Fork River, and kayaking on Lake Coeur d'Alene. Also offered is support for your own self-guided vacation, including full logistical support with luggage transfers, lodging, and shuttles when needed. ROW is headquartered in Coeur d'Alene, ID at 202 E. Sherman Avenue and is open Mon. to Fri., 9 a.m. to 5 p.m. National Geographic Adventure Magazine voted ROW Adventures one of the "Best Adventure Travel Companies on Earth."

TAXIS AND SHUTTLES

Captain Lou's Bicycle Shuttle Services–208.818.2254 (Based in Harrison, ID). Payless Airport–208.762.7433 (Minivans that accommodate up to 7 with cycles. Call to clarify rules about how to transport bikes & make pre-arrangements).
Spokane Airport Express–509.413.7986. They provide transport all around the region, so don't let the name fool you. They are willing to explore all cyclist transport needs. Prefer you call two days in advance, but will do shorter time if logistics allow.

BOAT TRANSPORT

HI Water Adventures–208.245.4517 (Boat shuttle on Lake CdA for people & bikes).

PUBLIC BUSES

Spokane Area Transit–509.328.RIDE (7433) www.spokanetransit.com.
CityLink–1.877.941.RIDE (7433) www.idahocitylink.com.
Greyhound–www.greyhound.com.

NOTE: *Services providers listed in **Bold** support this guide and/or related Web sites. Please consider them for your cycle vacation needs.*

THE BITTERROOT LOOP
Service Providers

Cycle Equipment Rental

Excelsior Cycles, Kellogg–208.786.3751
The Cycle Haus (formerly Pedal Pushers), Harrison–208.689.3436
Silver Mountain Sports Shop, Kellogg–208.783.1517
Friends of the Coeur d'Alene Trails, Wallace–413 Sixth St.
Lookout Pass–208.744.1301

Watercraft Rental

Harrison Pontoons and Rentals, Harrison–208.696.1770
HI Water Adventures, Harrison–208.245.4517

(Check with your lodgings provider to inquire about rental package deals).

Lodging and Camping–Trail of the Coeur d'Alenes

ACCOMMODATIONS WITHIN ONE MILE OF THE TRAIL

PLUMMER TRAILHEAD
    Hiway Motel & Sport Shop–208.686.1205
INDIAN CLIFFS & CHATCOLET TRAILHEAD
    Heyburn State Park–(Camping, Cabins & Cottages. RVs, Tents)–888.922.6743, 208.686.1308
LACON
    Crow's Nest Cottage–(Vacation Home, 2 day min.)–208.696.1770
HARRISON TRAILHEAD
    Cabin, The–(Vacation Home, 3 day min.)–208.661.8929
    City of Harrison Campground–208.689.3393 (Seasonal Host)–208.689.3212
    Corskie House B&B–208.689.9265
    Float Home–(Unique Floating Vacation Home on the CdA River)–208.660.2648
    Harrison House–(Vacation Home, 2 day min.)–208.696.1770
    Lakeview Lodge–(Motel)–208.689.9789
    Osprey Inn–(B&B)–208.689.9502
CATALDO TRAILHEAD
    Kahnderosa RV/Campgrounds–(RVs and Tents)–208.682.4613
    The Mission Inn–(Primitive tenting)–208.682.4435
PINE CREEK TRAILHEAD
    By the Way Campground–(Camping Cabin, RVs, and Tents)–208.682.3311
KELLOGG TRAILHEAD
    Guest House Inn & Suites–(Motel)–208.783.1234
    Kellogg Vacation Homes–800.435.2588
    Morning Star Lodge–(Silver Mt. Resort, rooms and suites)–866.344.2675
    Silverhorn Motor Inn–800.437.6437
    The Ridge–(Vacation Condos)–800.435.2588
    Trail Motel–208.784.1161
ELIZABETH PARK TRAILHEAD
    Crystal Gold Mine–(RVs)–208.783.4653

THE BITTERROOT LOOP
Service Providers

Lodging and Camping–Trail of the Coeur d'Alenes

OSBURN TRAILHEAD
  Blue Anchor RV Park–(RVs and Tents)–208.752.3443
WALLACE TRAILHEAD
  Brooks Hotel–208.556.1571
  Hercules Inn–(Vacation Rental Suites)–208.556.0575
  Stardust Motel–208.752.1213
  The Banker–(Vacation Home)–800.435.2588
  The Lux Rooms–(Boutique Hotel)–208.753.6001
  The Ryan Hotel–(Boutique Hotel)–208.753.6001
  The Wallace Inn–(Motel, Courtesy Shuttle)–800.643.2386
  Wallace RV Park–(Camping Cabins, RVs, and Tents)–208.753.7121
MULLAN TRAILHEAD
  Lookout Motel–208.744.1601
  Mullan House B&B–208.755.8547
  Mullan Trail–(Cabins, RVs)–208.744.1444

Lodging and Camping–Northern Pacific (NorPac)

LOOKOUT PASS
  Lookout Pass Ski & Recreation Area–(Self Contained RV)–208.744.1301

Lodging and Camping–Old Milwaukee Road

NORTH FORK ST JOE (Between Pearson Trailhead and Avery, Idaho)
  Telichpah Forest Service Campground–208.245.4517
AVERY, IDAHO
  Avery Gift Shop–(Vacation Suite)–208.245.1308, or 208.245.2055
  Avery Schoolhouse B&B (Opening summer of 2016)–208.245.2450
  Cabins by the Joe–Cabins, RV Camping–425.773.3725
  Scheffy's Hotel–208.245.4410
CALDER, IDAHO
  Calder Store–(RVs, Primitive Tenting)–208.245-2284
  Spring Creek–(Dry Cabins)–208.245.5268

Lodging and Camping–State Route Five

ST. MARIES, IDAHO
  Birch Tree B&B–208.245.2198 or 208.691.3696
  Fort Hemenway Manor–(B&B, Courtesy Shuttle)–208.245.7979
  River Front Suites–208.582.1724
  St. Joe Riverfront Bed & Breakfast–208.245.8687
  The Guest House–208.245.5755
  The Pines Motel–(Courtesy Shuttle) 208.245.2545

BETWEEN ST MARIES AND PLUMMER
  Alvin's Campground–(RVs, Tents, Camping Cabin)–208.245.5879
  Heyburn State Park, Benewah–(RVs, Tents)–208.686.1308
  Heyburn State Park, Hawley's–(Cottages, Cabins, RVs, Tents)–208.686.1308

THE BITTERROOT LOOP
Service Providers

Lodging and Camping-Other

OTHER ACCOMMODATIONS–MORE THAN A MILE OFF THE TRAILS

HARRISON MARINA TRAILHEAD

Grandma's Cabin–(Vacation Home on Trail). Mostly flat 5-mile ride on rural highway and lakeside road.–208.696.1770.

BULL RUN TRAILHEAD

Watson's Rose Lake Resort–(Vacation Apartment, Rustic Cabins, RV, Tenting). Mostly flat 2-mile ride on rural highway.–208.682.3604.

EAST PORTAL, ROUTE OF THE HIAWATHA

Mangold's General Store and Motel, Saltese, MT. Flat ride of 4.2 miles on multi-use trail.–406.678.4328

BETWEEN AVERY AND CALDER

Spring Creek Cabins–(Camping cabins). 2-mile flat ride on hwy.–208.245.5268

Connecting Trips: Trail of the Coeur d'Alenes

Connecting Trips present additional options for food, lodging, and/or recreation. These destinations are selected for their unique features or services, even though they are more than a mile from the Bitterroot Loop trails. All but one have lodgings on site or close by. To qualify as a Connecting Trip they must be:

1) Fun or intereseting.

2) Be accessiblesible by an easy, primarily flat ride from a trailhead, or, offer a courtesy shuttle or other transport option.

These Connecting Trips are listed by trailhead from west to east, (clockwise) on the Bitterroot Loop.

CHATCOLET TRAILHEAD

H2H Bison Ranch & RV Camp–(Dry Cabins, RV, Tipi, Tenting, Food Option, Courtesy Shuttle)–208.686.0108, h2hbisonranch.com

Sun Meadow Family Nudist Resort–(Motel Rooms, Cabin, RV, Tenting, Food, Courtesy Shuttle)–208.686.8686, sunmeadow.org

CATALDO TRAILHEAD

Coeur d'Alenes Old Mission State Park–(Historical Attraction)–208.682.3814 parksandrecreation.idaho.gov/parks/coeur-d-alenes-old-mission

ENAVILLE TRAILHEAD

Country Lane B&B Resort on the North Fork–(B&B, Cabin, RV, Tenting, Food, Courtesy Shuttle)–1.877.670.5927, countrylaneresort.com

SILVER MOUNTAIN TRAILHEAD

Silver Mt. Resort–(Gondola Ride, Mountain Activities, Lodging at Base, Food)–877.230.2193, *silvermt.com*

Government Offices

Coeur d'Alene Tribe–208.686.1800; Tribal Police–208.686.2050
Benewah County–208.245.3212; Sheriff, non-emergency–208.245.2555
Kootenai County–208.446.1000; Sheriff, non-emergency–208.446.1300
Shoshone County–208.752.1264; Sheriff, non-emergency–208.556.1114
Idaho Panhandle National Forests Headquarters–208.765-7233

EMERGENCY: DIAL 9-1-1

THE BITTERROOT LOOP
Roadside Attractions

- [ ] The Veterans' Memorial, Plummer Trailhead
- [ ] *Smoke Signals* Movie Location, Bobbi's Bar, Plummer
- [ ] Historic Mullan Military Rd., Heyburn State Park, Plummer
- [ ] Chatcolet Bridge, Heyburn State Park
- [ ] Longest Electrical Cable, Over South Lake Coeur d'Alene
- [ ] Old Harrison Jail, Crane Museum, Harrison
- [ ] Historic Building Walking Tour, Harrison
- [ ] Idaho's Oldest Building, Coeur d'Alenes Old Mission, Cataldo
- [ ] *Dante's Peak* Movie Location, Albert's Landing, Enaville
- [ ] Building Wearing a Miner's Hat, Kellogg
- [ ] North America's Longest Gondola, Silver Mountain, Kellogg
- [ ] Scrap Metal Sculptures, Kellogg
- [ ] WPA Historic Post Office Mural, Kellogg
- [ ] 1882 Underground Gold Mine, Crystal Gold Mine, Kellogg
- [ ] Sunshine Mine Disaster Memorial, Big Creek
- [ ] Captain John Mullan Statue, Wallace
- [ ] Center of the Universe, Historic Downtown Wallace
- [ ] *Dante's Peak* Movie Location, Historic Downtown Wallace
- [ ] *Heaven't Gate* Movie Location, Historic Downtown Wallace
- [ ] Historic Trolley Rides and Mine Tour, Wallace
- [ ] Last Stop Light in a Coffin, Wallace Mining Museum, Wallace
- [ ] Mining Display, Wallace Visitor Center, Wallace
- [ ] Pulaski Monument, Wallace
- [ ] Elmer's Fountain, along I-90 Near Mullan
- [ ] Captain John Mullan Statue, Mullan
- [ ] Avery Jail, Downtown Avery
- [ ] Milwaukee Dining Car, Downtown Avery
- [ ] Trout Pond, Downtown Avery
- [ ] Historic Logging Display, Marble Creek on the St. Joe River
- [ ] Captain John Mullan Statue, St. Maries
- [ ] Historic Murals, Downtown St. Maries
- [ ] Logger Memorial, Downtown St. Maries
- [ ] Paul Bunyan Statue, Downtown St. Maries
- [ ] Steam Donkey, Mullan Park, St. Maries
- [ ] Outer Space Tree, Hughes House, Downtown St. Maries
- [ ] World's Highest Navigable River, State Route 5
- [ ] Civilian Conservation Corps Projects, Heyburn State Park

34565168R00070

Made in the USA
Middletown, DE
26 August 2016